Listening for Their Voices

Jennifer Lawrence

Listening for Their Voices

Jennifer Lawrence

Hubbardston, Massachusetts

Asphodel Press
12 Simond Hill Road
Hubbardston, MA 01452

Listening for Their Voices
© 2014 Jennifer Lawrence
ISBN 978-1-938197-11-6

Cover photo © 2012 Graham Richter

All rights reserved. Unless otherwise specified,
no part of this book may be reproduced in any form
or by any means without the permission of the author.

Printed in cooperation with
Lulu Enterprises, Inc.
860 Aviation Parkway, Suite 300
Morrisville, NC 27560

To my mother, who has never stopped believing in me, no matter how far I have strayed from what mainstream society sees as "normal". Thank you for being accepting of the paths I had to walk.

*And to Himself:
Fjölnir, Ýjungr, Gangleri, Hrafnaguð, Sviðrir, Njótr, Óski, and (most of all) Haptaguð, who refuses to let me quit, no matter how hard the road.*

Contents

Voices From The North

Odin
- Odin's Call 1
- Odin On The Tree 3
- Bibliophile 7
- Force of Nature 9
- Surrender 11
- The Gift 13
- The View From The Well 14
- Courtship 16
- Checkmate 18
- Prayer of the God-þegn 20

Loki and His Family
- Necessary Evils 21
- Cold Stoneware 25
- Ironwood's Daughter 29

The Aesir
- Immortality 32
- Golden Delicious 34
- Sacrifice 36
- Lost Sweetness 39
- Hod's Confession 40

The Vanir
- Red Offerings 42
- Antler 43
- Aureate 46

Epics and Runes
- The Alfar 47
- Gudrun's Lament On Her Death-Bed 48
- In Utgard-Loki's Hall 51
- Answers (Ansuz) 54
- Gebo 56
- Hagalaz 59

    Isa 62
    Naudhiz 65

Ireland and the Celtic Lands
Brigid
    Red Flame 69
    Song to Brigid at Imbolc 70

The Morrighan
    Washerwoman 71
    Advice 72
    You Will Know Me 74

The Tuatha de Danann
    Keening 78
    Kingly 81
    Etain's Lesson 84
    Long-Armed, Many-Skilled 94
    Feral 97
    Cruinniuc's Folly 102
    Fuamnach's Accusation 106

Diverse Others
    Herne 110
    Night-Blooming 116

The Shores Of Greece
Hermes
    Gratitude 121
    Hermes At The Gate 122
    Hermes In America 124
    64 Adorations for Hermes 128
    Prayer to Hermes 130
    To Hermes Enodios 131
    All Your Faces 133

Demeter and Persephone
    Pomegranate 135
    Demeter's Kiss 137
    Persephone's Choice 138

For Demeter	142
To Demeter Erinys	143
Homecoming	145
My Persephone	147
Persephone's Dilemma	148

Athena

Hard Lessons	150
Visitation	151

Artemis

Lady Of The Cedars	153
The Death Of Actaeon	154

Dionysos

First Meeting	156
To Dionysus Lyaeus	158
Eleutherus	161

Other Olympians and Titans

Apology to Hekate	162
Written On The Waves	164
Adamant	165
Foam-Born	167
Hades' Lament	169
Homecoming II	171
Helios Grieves	173
Sun God's Crown	175
Teléia	176

Stories from the Wine-Dark Seas

Incandescent	178
Daedalus Regrets	180
Icarus	185
Calliope	186
Where She Went Wrong	188
No Distaff, No Loom	190
In The Wake Of The Maenads	192
Abhorred	194
Herakles Aboard The Argo	196

King Minos's Folly 198
ΚΑΛΛΙΣΤΗΙ 199

Other Tales

Broken Transformation 203
Child of Crow 204
Song For My Ancestors 205
Teind 207

Voices From The North

Odin's Call

Like the spider spinning his web in a high wind,
You were persistent, tapping again and again
At the door to my heart and head, until I listened,
Opened the door, and let you in.

I thought I had nothing to do with the gods of the North,
Preferring to walk another path, thinking my life
Already too complicated and confused to warrant
Following any others.

But you would not accept my refusal, sending
Little signs and omens: two ravens following
My car, a gray cat adopted on Wednesday who wanders
And will not shut up: so like you.

What need had I for your guidance? I was stubborn,
Did not want to take the steps to meet you,
Knowing how much you would demand of me,
Not knowing whether I could give it.

After a hard lifetime, I tend to think myself unworthy
Of such attention, and you confused me, chasing after
Me so relentlessly; I preferred to think I only imagined it,
Because what would you want with one such as myself?

I don't ask those questions any more—or if I do, I know
That, while I might not be able to answer them, you must
Have your reasons. Better, then, to serve you best as I can,
Though what gifts I have to offer are little enough.

These verses will win me no friends. Your followers are a
Bold and boasting lot, whereas I have always striven to be
Meek and mild, hiding my lights away, better to go unnoticed,

Better to avoid strife, sorrow, and conflict.

But hiding from you did not work, and so I am here,
Hoping that someday I will understand why you wanted me,
Knowing because you did that there must be more that I can offer
Than the nothing I believe myself to be.

Odin On The Tree

In the first light of dawn, Yggdrasil beckoned.

Branches spread out far above me,
Ropes dangling from every limb.
The bent servant I had brought along with me
Bore me aloft,
Bound me inescapably at a point
Too high to descend unaided,
And then lifted Gungnir
And transfixed me through with it,
From foot to head,
The foot-long blade of sharpest steel
piercing through near groin
and emerging 'twixt throat and collarbone
in a flood of gore.

I remember pain.
Even from that first day,
it was my constant companion,
And why should anyone expect otherwise?
No sacrifice can be called such
—is deserving of the name—
if pain and blood and fear are not its attendant midwives.

The tree stretched above me,
below me,
Extending upward, downward, outward
to pierce all the Nine Worlds,
Carrying the echoes of the screams I did not voice
to the ears of every soul—
Aes, Van, man, Alf, dwarf, Jotun—
that drew breath and set foot
against rock or soil.

Babes were born to the sound of my silent shrieks;
men died with the void of my unvoiced agony resonating in their ears.
Hunger and thirst did not sink their talons into me
until the second day,
Clawing at my guts,
racking me against the wooden frame that cradled me.
The sun scorched and blinded me by day; the cold
froze me at night; wilting and shaking by turns,
I forebore to yield.
Two dark shapes scythed through the sky above me,
wheeling in endless circles, their will bent
to Watch and Remember;
no greedy scavengers waiting for my final breath,
but guardians of my every observation and recollection.

They say time flies when one is having fun;
I can tell you the opposite is also true:
the days crept along more slowly than
the glaciers in Jotunheim, night following day
in a fashion both inexorable and ruthless.
I could feel my muscles shrivel, my tendons shrink,
and every spare ounce melted from my body;
no eagle came to feed me, though three times in the span of nights
in which I hung, clouds gathered and darkened, and
brought me rain to drink.
From the fourth day on, I was blessed and cursed with visions:
the sight of what was yet to come, foretold by the seer:
the sight which chills every man's soul—
the moment in which his life comes to an end.

Such sights! I shut them out,
willing a greater blindness for myself
than hunger and the dark of night could grant.
Such horrors, and to know that, in the end,
so little would remain.

I vowed to do what I could to forestall it,
and knew that those hideous visions would remain with me
after my time on the tree ended,
even if all else was lost.
This vow set me against Him I had chosen as brother,
set me, too, against His children,
and made it all but certain that the conflict that would ensue
could not be avoided.
In seeking to prevent it, I would bring it on;
and I found myself trapped
in the coils of a dilemma that could not be solved.

In the three days that followed upon this realization,
I howled until the cords within my throat
splintered and drove me to silence.
Even the wolves that ravened in the wilderness
around the tree's roots fled at that awful sound,
caring not to investigate the freshets of clotted gore
that issued from my ruined throat.
Nor did Ratatosk venture closer, nor
Nidhogg below emerge to question that terrible noise.

And on the eighth day, I rested.
No man and no god may evade his Wyrd,
and to make that attempt only tangles you
more tightly in its clutches. I hung limp,
quiet, the air barely stirring in my lungs,
the ouroboros coils of my fate writhing round me.

Slowly, where the drops of blood had burst forth
from the wound rent in my flesh, the soil began to stir,
each grain and particle moving as if carried by an ant.
I watched them shift themselves, change themselves,
bonding with my blood, the darker-stained bits rising to the top,
forming shapes upon the ground.

Fehu the first was, and Uruz that followed,
their strokes traced upon the earth in black and potent ichor.
Thurisaz and Ansuz next, their power in their sounds,
Raidho and Kenaz, Gebo and Wunjo,
their names whispered into my ears by they themselves,
the magic I had sought.
On their heels came Hagalaz and Naudhiz, Isa and Jera,
Eiwaz and Perthro, Elhaz and Sowilo:
the dire and the light,
with power to doom or to save, to shield or to slaughter.
Tiwaz, Berkano, Ehwaz and Mannaz,
Laguz and Ingwaz, Dagaz and Othala.
They lay before me like a treasure of fire-bright gems,
Gleaming all the more vividly as the sun rose on the morn
of the tenth day.

The ropes holding me snapped, and I fell screaming,
    without worry,
    without fear,
    without pain,
And landed on my feet like one of Freya's cats,
Heart thundering in my chest,
and dipped my hands down to gather them up.
I could feel the magic they bore within them—
mine, now
—and hid them away,
mind suddenly reeling with new plans,
plans of battle and strategy and survival,
and hurried away to begin.

The final time awaits.

Bibliophile

I know you watch me.
I can feel it, feel your gaze
No matter where I go, no matter if it is day or night,
No matter if I sleep or wake.
You are not the One who sends guardians to protect
Those who follow you
From the least little scratch, no;
You watch me like you'd keep your eye
On any minimally valuable thing you owned—
Not a house, or a car, or even the keys to such.
No, maybe like a book you'd read,
And enjoyed,
And might read again someday,
If the mood struck you
And you weren't overly busy.

I am no chieftain, no warrior,
No skilled craftsman;
The only skill I have is with words,
And that skill small enough, to be sure.
But nonetheless, you are—I hope—
Reluctant to give me up without good reason;
A man might, if he were generous,
Lend out a book he'd enjoyed,
To a friend he trusted,
But in the end, he would want it back,
And in no worse shape than when he lent it out.
And if it was lost? Destroyed?
Well, men have gone to war over less things,
Smaller insults,
Than the destruction of a book.

I sing no childish prayers before bed each night

Asking you to protect me;
As if even your protection would divert my Wyrd;
But I might, when I lay down to sleep, eyes closed,
Not knowing whether I will wake in the morning or not,
Whisper thanks to you for the gift of the day I have had,
Even if it was wretched, I am glad it was not worse,
And promise to greet you again on the morrow if I wake,
And if not,
Then your book will come back to its shelf again at last,
Ready to share its stories and verses with you once more.

Force of Nature

Like the glaciers that conquer every mountaintop in the lands where
He was first worshipped,
like ancient snow frozen hard as steel, rasping over the peaks,
like ice grinding away stone,
He stands above all, immovable, obdurate,
And when He wills it,
    nothing may stand in His way,
    or block His path,
    or thwart His desires.
He knows the patience of ages,
His schemes span centuries, waiting for this piece or that
to fall into place so He may play it against His foes.
He does not flinch at the toppling of soaring pinnacles,
nor move away if some minor and momentary inconvenience
causes Him annoyance.
Against His will, all obstacles fall, all barriers burst asunder:
steel is not so strong, stone not so hard,
and the chasm of decades falling away to dust not so vast.
Always a dozen steps (or more) ahead
of those who would see Him fail,
He plots His course with meticulous care
and infinite, boundless persistence.
Blessed with the foresight to see the future unfolding
—the eye given up for such a boon, small loss—
He can outwait seeming failures,
and in the end they are revealed
as triumphs, after all.
No man, no Alf, no Van, and no Aes may withstand
the unrelenting force of his vision and his power,
and in the end,
the will of those who might try
is ground away, just as the glaciers grind away stone,

by His will,
> inescapable,
> inexorable,
> unavoidable,
> inevitable.

Surrender

Did I ever have a choice?
A true chance to keep the things I held dear,
The one I called beloved,
My safe and quiet life?
Or was it fated that my crutches would be kicked away
From the first moment I came under Your scrutiny?
Were those seeds of dissatisfaction
Planted in him that long ago?

When a person is wounded and the wound festers,
Sometimes the only way to be healed is to cut away the rot
before it poisons body and soul.
Long have I known that the ancestors sang Your name
Over their charms to mend flesh and purge poisons:
And so You became the scalpel.
Surgery always hurts:
Though drugs or grief may mask the agony for awhile,
in time the flesh and spirit
remember that torture and must face it, accept it, for it to heal.
Such wounds leave scars,
Marks on body and soul that never fade:
A map to show us and others
    how we've suffered,
      when we keened out our pain,
      and what we survived.

Defying You is a losing battle, this I know;
But in me is still some kernel of rebellion,
Some illusion that I have free will,
that my Wyrd is not set in stone.
And still: belief eludes me—
raised in a doubting and doubtful age,
I question whether what I suspect

and what I fear is true.

I agreed to be Your skald,
But I cherished the thought that I still owned myself.
Now this belief is crumbling,
And my last vestige of hope,
of fear, of disbelief
pleads with me to proclaim
    that this is fantasy
      this no more than a nightmare that will pass,
    this but a product of a sick and unstable mind,
that it is all in my head.
Even after staring at the runes I have drawn
—*Ansuz Jera Sowilo*
Uruz Fehu Berkano
Isa Dagaz Laguz—
I still want to deny what I know to be true,
But denial fades fast in the face
of all that You are.

So I shall uproot myself from my sheltered, shattered grove,
and allow myself to be transplanted;
I shall cease to mourn my old garden, now lost to me,
and plant leeks alongside the ash tree in my new one.
I shall hang images of cattle and stags on the walls
of the new home You will lead me to.

And I will write Your songs and prayers,
And I will tend my cats in Freya's name,
And I will till the soft soil for Nerthus,
And honor my ancestors,
And praise the wights of land and house,
And hold blot for the Alfar,

And do Your bidding.

The Gift

This is what I offer You:
Your mark, burned into my skin,
The wound rubbed with ointment
of bear fat and henbane and ashes,
The better to urge the scar to run deep,
Deep as Your hooks in my heart.
As true a brand and lasting
As those ranchers sear into the hides of cattle—
Save, in this case,
The cow did it to herself.

This is what You give me:
The severance of my ties to the one
I once held most dear,
The better to serve You,
No matter how much I bleed,
No matter how much I weep,
No matter how much I wail and beg and scream.
No more distractions from Your work:
A kingly gift, indeed.

This is my gift to You:
Everything.
What else have You left me?
In time, I will learn not to resent it,
And see it as the blessing You mean it to be.
No matter how I whimper,
No matter how much I sob,
No matter how much I tremble alone in the night.
A gift fit for a god—
And, as such, the only thing I have
Worthy of You.

The View From The Well

How odd, to realize
that as that fleshy orb sunk slowly down
through the sky-clear waters,
I could still see it:
depth was no bar to my perception, nor darkness.
Moreover, that detached organ
could itself still see—
as if, trailing that severed nerve,
those pale, gristly cords still reached out,
connected, ghost-like,
across the inches, feet, yards—
(worlds)
—that separated us, to where I stood.

Atop my high seat in Valaskjálf
I can scry across nine worlds,
But my eye in the well
sees only into me, and all that I do:
    claiming fallen warriors,
    planning machinations,
    moving my game pieces—
all actions meant to delay the inevitable.
I am in this for the long haul,
and there are those who, behind closed doors,
mutter
(as if I cannot hear!)
about the dishonor my deeds bring upon me.

Bullshit.

There is no dishonor in killing a foe,
seducing a woman,
plotting betrayal,

weaving such a Wyrd-web
as even the Norns might envy.
All I do, I do for the greater good,
the final end,
and to that end I have sacrificed much:
> my eye
>
> my son
>
> myself.

Do you think, then, that I would quibble
at rearranging the lives of a few mortals?

If I could leave them untouched and still
achieve the same end, I might;
And then, I might not?
Who knows?
Even I cannot always see the outcome of my plans,
or the consequences of my acts:
After all, it is sometimes very hard
to see things from the bottom of a well.

Courtship

This is not inspired wooing;
When I asked you that you take away the pain
of loving one who does not love me,
I did not realize that you would do so by
driving me to self-violence,
then have him imprison me for my own good.
I did not know that you would try to make me hate him.
Perhaps I should have, but you have many wives,
and it is the god of the Israelites who
claimed to be a jealous god;
Nowhere in the lore does it say that you are jealous,
though the myths recount that you are treacherous,
> a liar,
> not to be trusted,
> manipulative, and...
well, we all have our own flaws, do we not?

I have said repeatedly that I want nothing to do
with being your bride,
that such is far too much madness for even
my broken soul to tolerate.
But you do not listen,
just repeatedly press your suit.
I do not want this; I had a love I was happy with,
but such was no obstacle to you;
you tore him away from me,
shaped his mind like you would shape a spell or rune,
and in doing so,
tore the living heart from my chest.
How I survive, I do not know;
Perhaps over the years,
I have simply learned to live with pain,
no matter how great;

how to endure the most awful torments
and still go on breathing.
And perhaps I only imagine it, after all,
and I am dead, and have entered Hel's realm.
This might be preferable
to being wed to You.

Then again, what else have you left me?
Bring on the musicians.
Set the table.
Pour the mead.
Let the bridal dance begin.
It is not as though anyone else would want me,
or could have me,
now that you have made your claim,
now that you have begun to break me and remold me
into the shape you have decided is best for me.
My will, my choices
never entered into it,
so do not be too surprised
when you find the bridal bed
a cold and lonely place, indeed—
Empty as the place where
my heart once beat.

Checkmate

And in the end, You will still win.

In the belly of the beast,
Swallowed whole by Fenrir's massive maw,
You endure, adamant against
the searing fluids that seek to
break You down and digest You;
But there is no will more iron than Yours;
there is no strength of mind and soul stronger than Yours.

And when the battle is done,
    When Víðarr has slain the ravening wolf and gone away,
    When the battlefield lays strewn
        with the remains of the mighty Aesir
        and the shining Vanir,
Two ravens will drop down
from the unimaginable heights
where they have waited
and alight on the wolf's bulging belly,
Thought and memory watching
as that grey-furred flesh stretches,
drawn taut by a dagger's point,
And then splits wide to reveal You,
Old man,
grinning savagely,
One eye sparkling with bloody mirth,
and that air of satisfaction
hanging on You like a heavy, dark cloak
as You climb from the body of Your dead killer,
ancient shaman once again having died and
been reborn into the world from the belly of death.

You will reach down to the ground

that is a sea of red mud churned up in the battle
with the blood of gods and giants alike,
take up Gungnir from where it fell,
pluck Your filthy hat from the wound
from whence You crawled,
and laugh in victorious exultation as—
Your greatest scheme come to a triumphant end,
all machinations finished—
You head off to wander once more,
Two knifelike, feathered shapes trailing You
as they follow You down the road,
Faithfully accompanying You as You set out
on Your next adventure.

Prayer of the God-þegn

So, then:
I acknowledge I am owned.
Haptaguð, fetter-god,
You hold my chains.
You placed the collar around my throat.
I do not act without your approval,
I do not speak without your permission.

It is a wise man, and a wiser god,
who knows how best to treat his property.
Mistreat it, strain it, stress it,
and any tool will break.
Use it for a purpose it is unsuited to,
and you destroy it—
And then, what point in claiming a tool at all?

A wise man, and wiser god,
is no child, careless or malicious,
to break a toy simply for the joy of
seeing it break—
and You are no child.
Karl, I know you own me,
know I do not even breathe unless you will it,
But I plead for you to use me gently:
You have put me under so much strain already,
I fear to break.
Still, I am yours:
to wield or for woe—
Do as you will.

Necessary Evils

"The finest steel is that which goes through the hottest fire."
The man called himself a Quaker,
but he understood me well enough:

I count my existence in moments of rage
interspersed with eons of agony—
the shorter ones, I can barely hear each drop of venom
splashing into the bowl over my shrieked imprecations,
before those sweeter sounds are replaced with screams
as my eyes burn in their sockets with a fire
greater even than that of Surt's blade, buried in a man's heart.
Those motes of time seem longer than the ones that bracket them,
fore and aft: each roar in which I feel only
the vile liquid scorching away my sight,
giving me visions that my beloved blood-brother
could only hope to achieve.

For I see the end:
chains broken, terror and panic as inevitable change tears its way
through the old and stagnant world, demolishing stale customs
and outmoded ways as easily as a child topples a tower of toy blocks.
This is the gift I have been given, forged like finest steel
in the crucible of raving torture;
No matter how the one-eyed wanderer seeks to find a way
to prevent what will come, still it *will* come.
They don't understand it, those cowering children,
bound by their ways as surely as I lie bound underneath the earth
with the bowels of my son; bound by their fears as I am bound
to lay here, anticipating each drop, each soft wail from my wife
as she goes to empty the overfull bowl,
the poison slopping over the brim
to sear her fingers.

Long have they hated me for my machinations,
ignoring the gifts those plans have resulted in;
so, too, do they hope to ignore—to avert—
the final gift I bring: the gift of change.
Of rebirth.
They think only of their own lives,
their own domains, their own halls,
willing to sacrifice any number of souls to avoid
the unavoidable.

"Any change is resisted because bureaucrats have a vested interest
    in the chaos in which they exist."

Oh, he was a bright one, that hated man—hated
by the people he led, all so willing to pillory him for his mistakes—
and, yes, he made them, as what man (or god)
does not?
And those who hounded him from his seat of power
were all too ready to ignore
the gifts he brought them, the changes he ushered in,
even though they celebrate those changes now,
(easily forgetting who brought them).
Even as I scream, even as I howl, even as I rage,
I do not forget:
this is my crucible; here all dross is burned away,
    leaving only my indomitable will,
    leaving only raw purpose.
    leaving only that inevitable future.
Nothing can prevent it:
    not the prayers of man,
    not the plans of the gods,
    not all the hopes or fears of both.

There are others in the world who understand the role
of those like me much better than those

who condemn me so;
to the east and south, a land where the people have always
    worshipped gods and goddesses in multitudes,
just as once we were;
and among their greatest and most high are three:
one to create, one to preserve,
and one to destroy the old, that it may be replaced with the new.
He who destroys is venerated as necessary,
without which there can be no balance between old and new,
and who fights ignorance and fear as his greatest foe.
Would that those who worship my brother and his kin
    understood me so well!

Your physicists see a part of it:
the universe tends toward entropy,
and all things, once created, wind down toward extinction,
either pushed there or pulled there
by the forces of age, use, and decay.
But I suppose it is useless
to expect more from those who claim to look forward to death
and the opportunity to serve in the halls of Asgaard
when it is so much more obvious
that they tremble with fear of the final end
and uncertainty that anything at all comes
after their eyes have closed for the last time.

Do not misunderstand: I ask for nothing—
    not your comprehension,
    not your worship,
    not your love.
Such things might be sweet,
but I can exist without them,
    can withstand the fire that blazes
    within the hollows of my eye sockets,
    can withstand the hate and fear aimed my way

by those to whom I have brought gifts,
  too many times to count;
  can withstand the lack of hospitality,
  the jeers of scorn, the revulsion.
I can rise above it all, fueled by my conviction,
  knowing I am right,
  knowing I do what I do for the world itself,
  regardless of those who would stop me,
  knowing above all that there will come a time
    when the serpent is dead
    when the bowl is shattered
    when I walk free,
And then the world will see:
  this is necessary for survival.
Let the world of gods and men call my acts evil;
their opinions mean less to me
than the fire that burns away my weakness,
leaving behind the righteousness necessary
to do what must be done.
Soon, very soon,
  I
  will
  rise.

"Out of suffering have emerged the strongest souls;
the most massive characters are seared with scars."

Cold Stoneware
(For Galina)

How it is that your hands do not shake
as you hold the bowl,
you will never know.
It is impossible to look away:
> to shift your gaze from your beloved's contorted face,
> from the massive, heaving form of the serpent coiled above,
> from the ancient, broken stalactite its length is knotted around,
> and from the bowl of plain, unglazed crockery
> you hold in ever-steady hands.

Each drop of sizzling venom adds to the bowl's terrible freight;
each drop collects at the tip of the monster's fangs,
hesitates
(as if it is as reluctant to leave its maker
as you are to leave your heart's-twin)
and then falls into the murky lake in the bowl.
The stench is unbearable—
a chemical stink that burns your nostrils,
making you blink back tears,
but you would welcome the stink and the searing pain
if only it drowned out that other stench
(for, turned to iron now, the rotting entrails that
bind your beloved to the stone still reek—O, Narvi!)
—but it does not.
The minutes creep by with terrible slowness:
The bowl takes forever to fill,
but at the same time,
it fills all too quickly—
a deeper pain, for when it is full,
you must rise to empty it, and
step away from Him who is your world.

And then, as you hurry away to let the poison
pour from the bowl—for you cannot simply
empty it close to where he is bound;
the vapors would gather and kill you both—
His voice rises in agonized shrieks,
cursing those who bound Him,
and cursing you for leaving.
The serpent's venom does not cease to fall
just because you step away:
that is part of His punishment—
and yours.
And it is punishment;
as His wails and screams rise in intensity
with every step you take away from Him,
you feel an answering agony throughout
the whole of your form,
and most fixed, fierce, and shattering within your heart.
But no matter the pain you feel,
it does not crush you,
and you hurry back to His side
—bowl empty—
as swiftly as you can, taking your seat and
lifting the bowl into place again.
His eyes have gone milky from the venom,
and weeping scarlet sores crater His skin,
marring His once-smooth face,
but in the hours it takes for the bowl to fill again
—(and oh! how your arms ache and tremble and shake
at the strain of holding it in place for so long)—
they will heal; that is part and parcel
of this cruelty against Him.
For if those wounds did not vanish,
eventually the venom would burn away His nerves,
and there would be numbness,
and permanent surcease from the pain,

and you know that they have decided that
this would not do.
You would do anything to spare Him this,
such is your love for Him
(a love no less strong than that of his blood-brother
for his mistletoe-murdered son);
you would gladly take His place, if it was allowed.
But you know that, if you were to interpose your slender
frame between him and the snake, the serpent would
strike and slay you, casting your dead weight aside,
and then your love would have no one
to bear the burden of the bowl.

So you persevere, despite your grief;
    you persevere, despite your fear;
    you persevere, despite your anguish;
    you persevere, despite the fury that boils
within every particle of your body at this outrage.
You endure for Him whom you love,
for that is the heart and essence of love:
whatever your suffering, it is the only gift
you still have to give to Him, and such a poor gift,
so small and pathetic, so insufficient a recompense
for all the joy He has given you—
But it is all you have left, and it will have to do.

So you hold the bowl, smelling the phantom and lingering
stench of your dead son
(just one of the gifts that He who loves you gave to you),
smelling the reek of the snake's lethal venom,
feeling the burning ache begin to build in your arms
as the weight of the bowl begins to grow.

You hold the bowl, and you weep in joy at being
allowed to do this for Him, and weep in grief

for the joy you know no more
at the world you once had,
and then lost;
you hold the bowl, and weep in impotent rage against
those who have done this to Him.

Whatever may come, you hold the bowl.

Ironwood's Daughter

What is this shadow that walks behind me?

I emerged from the womb full-blooded as most do;
Ten fingers, ten toes, and a lusty squall
as I stole my first lungs'-suck of air:
and after that, the silent companion, ever with me:
swimming at my side that day I went out
past the deep-water marker in the Big Muddy at age 6;
holding the ladder for me when I was 10
and brushed a thumb against the metal screw
as I tried to change a lightbulb on my own;
watching from the corner as a friend's maddened dog
leapt for my throat and got his maws full only of
my elbow, hastily erected to block his fangs.
Since that first day I have lived
half in this world, half in the other,
suspended at the threshold,
And finding myself all too keen to learn
what takes place beyond that doorstep.

What is this shadow that walks beside me?

I am older now, have seen many a passing
of those who left me behind to mourn:
father, grandmother, grandfather, uncle, second mother,
and uncounted other ancestors who came and went
long before my birth and left me their blessings
but no memories of their names.

Nor have my own brushes ebbed:
astride a steel horse galloping in the rain
that slipped, taking a corner too swiftly,
and took me down with it;

plunging off the deep end of that hostel's swimming pool,
reaching for a handful of water to drag myself forward,
and feeling it slip through my fingers, claiming a lungful instead;
nearly mistaking foul herb for sweet one, and only the decision
to wait until I had taken my harvest home to wash it,
seeing the purple spots and smelling that odor of mouse,
kept me from writhing out my life in spastic dance on the floor.

Nor has that silent companion left my side:
I feel her presence, though I can almost but not quite see Her,
as I make my way from past to future.

What is this shadow that stands in front of me?

Dark days became darker, led me down shadow roads:
the unearthing of dead things, communing with their spirits,
claiming those relics still salvageable:
> antler and ash,
> fur and feather,
> bone and breath and blood.

I can strip a carcass flesh from bone in minutes,
keep my guts' contents inside me no matter how foul the stench,
feel the dance of maggots over my hands as I lovingly collect the
> corpses,

and feel You draw ever closer: watching, perhaps in curiosity,
seeing if I have learned my lessons:
Your lessons.

I draw them in as you draw them in—not as slaves,
but to send them on to where they belong: to rest, to return, to rise
Or to linger and spend time in sweet and quiet conversation
and gratefully accepting what wisdom they have to share.

Have I made myself interesting? Too interesting?
Bah, I do not delude myself

that I might die a warrior's death: I am skald, farmer, mother;
ill-health has trailed me all my life,
and if I do not die of sickness,
I will live long to die old,
and thereby still come to you.

But it is the final mystery that drives me, that need to know
which all things that draw breath seek to unravel:
what happens when our clay grows cold
and our bosom is no longer moved by our breath.
What is it like in that undiscovered kingdom:
Your kingdom?
Do we plunge down deep, full fathom five,
where light nor warmth nor affection kindle any spark?
Or, as some say, do You embody all those things in yourself?

I know what they say of you:
Face divided, half beauty, half putrescence,
And who would dare to kiss those lips?
I am not half in love with easeful death—not yet—not much—
and yet I know when my time comes,
there will be no turning aside; whether yet that fear lingers,
as it does with so many,
or whether I have at last bested that final remnant of mortality,
still will I turn to you, my silent companion
and walk respectfully, lovingly at your side
through the gates at the root of the tree
into that place which You call home.

What is this shadow that now stands before me,
    and holds out a skeletal hand in welcome?

Immortality

You've all heard that verse:
"Cattle die, kinsmen die…"
I'll let you in on a secret:
Odin heard it from me first.
The lot of us, sitting and passing around the horn,
Seeing which of us could come up with the most wisdom.
In the middle of all those couplets
About hard work and modesty,
And storing enough food for hard times
And not drinking overmuch when a guest at another's hearth
And not acting as if you know everything—
All those words about solid, humble, mortal concerns
(Such practical, common-sense matters)
—Suddenly, the secret of immortality?

You must understand:
Everything dies.
This is the sole immutable fact of the universe:
And not just yourself;
In the end, everything you have ever loved,
Will ever love,
Could ever love,
Will be stolen from you by the tyrant that is Time.
And although we watch from Asgard
As you spin out the centuries,
Making advances in science and slowly
Adding to your lifespans—
From thirty years to forty,
Forty years to fifty,
Sixty, seventy, eighty, ninety,
Even a hundred years—
To us, you are already dead and dust,
And have joined the ranks of your ancestors.

So do them proud,
Do *us* proud:
Tell your children the stories of your father,
Your grandmother,
And all those who came before them,
And know that they and their children
Will likewise tell such stories about you, someday.

It is my bride's gift to bring youth and new life—
Immortality, at least until Ragnarok
—to us here on Asgard,
And it is my gift to you of Midgard
To teach you the only way to life eternal
You will ever know.

So pour the mead,
Tell a story
Boast
    and brag
And honor my name
—and your own.

Golden Delicious

"An apple a day keeps the doctors away."
I taught you that, I with my basket full of radiant sweetness,
Sweetness I couldn't share with you;
Sweetness only for Odin and the Aesir,
Njord and his kin.

How can I explain it?
My love gave me no children,
Not over all the long years,
And so the ardor I would have lavished on daughters and sons
Instead went to the gnarled trees and their shining fruit.
I wept over every wind-broken bough,
Every squirrel-gnawed orb,
Every leaf blighted with rust.

A mother raises up her sons and sends them off,
To a king's hall to serve, and sometimes to die in battle;
Daughters she raises to serve another way,
And sometimes, they too die, bringing forth their own children
In bloody battle with themselves.
My children I carried close to my heart,
The basket I bore them in carved of ash wood—
Clean and smooth, holding no hidden taint within
To rot that precious treasure.

Each shining globe I take down from the branches that bear it
Only when its time has come, ripe and succulent and ready to fall
With the feather-kiss of the southern breeze.
I nurture the trees as best I can, bringing water and the fertilizer made
    by Odin's mount,
And trimming away the branches of any other trees nearby
That would grow too broad and encroach upon their domain,
Shutting out Sunna's brightness.

But no matter how much I love them,
How I tend them, how long I carry them,
Eventually the time comes
When I, too, must watch my children die;
Worse, I myself give them over to their murderers,
Pressing each smooth-skinned babe
Into the knotted hands of their killers,
And watching, unblinking, as they lift the apples to their mouths
And bite deep.

When the slaughter is finished,
I once again return to the orchard,
And with my own tears water the trees that will once again—
When next summer comes, bright and beautiful—
Entrust their children to me, their betrayer,
To die.

Sacrifice

There was never any doubt.
No chain smithed by mortal man would hold the eternal hunger,
And so—as so many times before—we turned to the dwarves
For the fetter to bind that malicious maw.
They crafted it out of six impossible things,
And told us: It will hold.
We knew Fenris could not snap this bond.

But so did He.

And so the Ravener asked:
By what token am I to trust in this game—
That, once bound, you will free me?

All of us, Aesir and Vanir, knew without speaking that,
Once our word was given, we would have to break it.
He could not be freed.
And I could see in their eyes that none of them—
Not the one-eyed wanderer,
Not the red-bearded thunderer,
Not the lord of the fertile fields,
Not the keen-eyed far-seer—
Would do so.

No, there was never any doubt.
In my mind, there was only certainty:
I do this thing because it must be done.
I do this thing because the Hunger must be bound.
I do this thing because there is no one else to do it.

Without hesitation, I told the baleful beast:
I, Tyr, will place my hand between your jaws.
If you are not freed when the game of binding is ended,

Then my oath is broken,
And my hand is forfeit.

He accepted this, for were not my unbroken word
And my good right hand—my sword-hand—
Ample token of trust?

I thrust my sword-hand between the beast's slavering jaws,
Felt those fangs—black with the rotting shreds
Of a thousand good warriors' hearts—close about the bones of my
    wrist.

And so they bound him: with woman's beard
And mountain's roots; with cat's footfall
And bird's spittle; with bear's sinews
And the breath of a fish—
Knowing beyond a doubt that it would hold.

And so did He.

I do this thing that must be done:
Let all men know by the hand I will lose that
    Tyr broke his oath.
I do this thing that must be done:
Let all men know by the hand I will lose that
    Tyr cared enough to make the sacrifice that had to be made.
I do this thing that must be done:
Let all men know by the hand I will lose that
    only by Tyr's will was the wolf bound.

I stared into the wolf's wild and wicked eyes as his fangs
sheared through the flesh and bone of my wrist,
slamming shut with a ghastly clash.

All the world could see the wolf's woe: I had won.

I, oath-broken.
I, the sacrifice.
I, wolf's bane.

The wolf howled in impotent rage and grief.
And I—bloody, broken, but not beaten—smiled.

Lost Sweetness

I long for the taste of apples:
that first sharp crunch,
the sweet juice filling my mouth,
the perfume lifting up to fill my nostrils.
In older times, they believed an apple would heal all ills,
and in my malaise, I could wish it were true.
I crave Idunn's gentle and feather-light healing touch.

I am old, old before my time, older than my years,
worn down and broken with grief and woe,
with ills enough for half a score of strong men, and—
were I a horse—
should have been put down as a mercy long ago.

My memory is fading, and these days, I forget much,
but I still remember the long-lost sweetness of summer apples.
and hunger for them as a woman with child
hungers for the strangest of meals,
and I mourn for the vanished savor of those fruits,
spangled with August morning dew,
their golden skin gleaming like the light of dawn
that caresses them.

I long in vain, of course.
Never again will I be blessed to feel that
smooth, sun-warmed weight of Idunn's gift in my hand,
enraptured by the tempting possibilities of a youth
that no longer lies waiting before me.
And never again will I sink my teeth into
that ivory flesh and purr in delight as
that perfect sweetness lingers on my lips.

Hod's Confession

It was only when I heard his mother scream
that I realized how
the Lie-Smith had tricked me.

I let the bow fall
from fingers grown suddenly numb and cold,
and reached out blindly
(as always);
    now I could hear the sound of running feet;
    now I could hear the Thunderer's furious roar;
    now I could hear women's' voices raised in wails of grief.
I could still smell the tart, bitter scent
of the freshly-hewn mistletoe sprig
the Mocker had brought and bound to the arrow's shaft
to serve as its head;
its thin, sticky sap oozed from the
sharply-splintered end of the twig.
There was a black flower of cold slowly blooming
in my chest, enfolding leaden petals
over my heart and lungs and guts.

I knew the blame would not fall entirely upon me,
but also on he who had brought the bolt, he
who had guided my hand.
Nonetheless, mine were the fingers that plucked the string,
and mine was the palm that grasped the bow;
weregild demanded I pay the price:
a life for a life.

It did not matter; the guilt was mine,
in knowing the devious one's spite of us all
and letting him provide and aim the weapon for me anyway.
I turned, leaving behind the broken sobs and the sound of battle

as they beat him to the ground.
Baldr the Beautiful was gone to Hel's kingdom,
a route no man or god returns from.
All this had risen from my desire to take part in the games,
from my plaintive plea.

Hodr the Blind I have always been,
but in the few short hours left to me, henceforth I shall never again
let the words I voice be used to bring ruin upon another.
I know they will soon send one to end me,
but henceforth I will be Hod the Silent, as well,
and let these be my final words:
I am sorry, brother.
Would that it had been me, instead.

Red Offerings

They tell me you like strawberries,
So I bring you a gift of them:
One cultivated, one wild.
Bright and ripe, sweet and fresh—
Like you.
No one has told me
You also like roses,
But still I see you with them
In my mind.
I know not why; so far
As I know, roses do not grow
In the northlands.
But still, I thought of you
And there I was,
Drowning in the richness of that smell.
So I bring you the gift of a rose, too—
Born wild, transplanted to my garden,
Red and small and sweet,
But its thorns no less sharp
For all of that.

Antler

Wandering the woods and
Foraging through forests to feast;
I feared no one, for none could defeat me:
Bold, brave, and brawny, I bested them all.

Then into my world stepped my bane;
He traded his sword for a bride,
and so sought out a new weapon
with which to smite the foe
And so, found me.

King of stags, I roamed the Hibernian hills,
content to traverse my range, sow my seeds,
eat, sleep, and fight my rivals.
And oh! Those fights!

None could match me for weight;
the breadth of my shoulders,
the roll of my flanks,
the dew that dappled my shaggy head,
spangled my fur,
and left a shine on my ever-sharp hooves.
There was no other hart
to match me, and so for a score of years,
I reigned, defeating all comers who sought
to steal my mates, winning every challenge.

And then He came.

There was no man or god to match him,
in lustiness or might;
the sun's light gleamed no more golden
than his hair, nor could any surpass

the length of his stride,
the fury of his battle-roar,
or the strength of his hands.

He sought me out in my realm,
and as I turned to face him, he charged,
his bellows echoing from hill to hill.
I met his charge with my own,
the earth flying in huge clods under my hooves,
skinned from the breast of the hill with each stride,
intending to rend him from crotch to craw with my antlers.

He surprised me, leaping at the last second
over my lowered head, twisting in his leap,
seizing my crown, and less than half a breath later,
I felt his weight atop my back.

I am no horse, to be ridden; my roar shook the trees,
but his grasp was too strong to shake loose,
and slowly, he began to force my head aside.

I ran.
    Ran, and felt my head twisting;
    ran, and felt the muscles of my neck and shoulders protesting;
    ran, and yet could not shake him off.

I was brought to a stop by a crash
that shattered the world,
and a bright white pain
that vanished as swiftly as morning mist.
He tossed himself from my back as my knees buckled
and I fell, crumbling, to the ground.

All was fading around me, but I had a last moment
of melting satisfaction that I had finally been bested

by one truly worthy of the honor.
Then he grasped one of my huge and branching antlers
and tore it from my brow.

A weapon fit for a god,
honorably won from a king.
My legend will live on.

Aureate

There is nothing about you that is not precious:
Bright-maned one,
Brisingamen shining round your alabaster throat,
The feather-cloak thrown 'cross your shoulders,
each pinion rippling in the wind.
No docile dolly, you!
You soar wrapped in
Sunna's brightness,
Fierce as the falcons that gave of themselves
to make up your treasure.
Amber and honey you love:
Tree-gold and bee-gold in abundance,
And mead poured out to honor you.
There could be no greater beauty,
and in recognizing this, I pay you
only one tiny portion
of the honor you are due.
However, I pray you accept this prayer
as the beginning of the gifts I owe you,
and beg your patience
Until I can bring forth the full flower
of the offerings you are due.

The Alfar

No prancing point-winged pastel pixies, we!
But warriors of the land, both wild and free!
With sword and spear, we fight at Volund's side,
And with bright Freyr's forces we shall ride.
There is no jotun, ettin, wyrm, or troll
That comes away from battle with us whole;
Of our halls' hospitality, skalds sing;
Our mead is fit for hero, Aes, or king.
Across the farthest borders we can see
Our foes as endless as the ocean's tide
And ready as the spider's jaws, we bide
To scythe them all away for Hela's fee.
Our fighters number as the blades of grass:
And while we stand, no foe shall ever pass.

Gudrun's Lament On Her Death-Bed

When was I not most wretched of women?
Woe I have worn like a woven wool wrap.
Nine griefs I have known, pain everlasting:
As many as nights Odin hung from the tree.

Sigurd—my sweetness, my only solace—
Slain by my mother's son; heavy my heart.
Husband hewn down by blood-bonded brother,
Who listened to lies from his own lady-love.

Doughty was he, the slayer of dragons,
But deeply bit the blades of his brothers—
Bound them by oaths and the blood of his bride;
Bitter the tears, when finally they fell.

Through woods and wastelands I wailed 'long the way;
For seven half-years was a stranger to kin;
When I returned, 'twas only to find a
Fate even fouler than before I faced.

Gunnar, my brother, hacked down in the hall
Of Atli the traitor, whose bloodied blade
Shaped scarlet slaughter, then wended to worse:
Unwillingly was I to that warrior wed.

Nor was it enough, this black-hearted beast
Should butcher one brother in vengeance bleak;
To avenge his sister, Brynhild the liar,
Högni the hero he hacked down as well.

I vowed I would never willingly yield;
Hate in my heart grew hard like a hammer;
And instead of porridge, pudding, or pork

For supper, his sons served to him in a pie.

Eitil and Erp, Atli eager to eat,
After the repast, the ruse I revealed;
But their blood was my blood, their bones mine too,
And what mother never mourns her sons' sad loss?

No more could I take; not if the gods begged
Me; into the sea with stones in my arms.
I hurled myself, hoping for death's mercy,
But instead a new home and husband soon found.

Svanhild, my daughter and Sigurd's so sweet,
Wooed by Eormenric, but wrongly accused:
He haled her as faithless, broken their bond,
And broken by horses in turn, she was slain.

Three sons I had by Jónakr of Sweden:
Bold Hamdir, brave Erp, and Sörli the Strong;
To Oium they went, sister to avenge;
They struck down the king, oath-broken so long.

But each one I lost; Erp to his brothers;
A misunderstanding led him to his *wyrd*.
The others laid low by loathsome lord's men;
And once more, time comes my children to mourn.

Beloved husband, children I have lost—
O sons, oh my daughter—with your absence, how
Shall I keep enduring when you are long gone?
Lonely is my deathbed, without your dear shades.

Soon shall I dwell in Hela's dark hall;
For now the darkness comes to my door;
Even in death, know I no joy or peace;

For the Choosers take my family from me.

Valkyries bear away husbands and sons;
To Odin or Freya all warriors go.
Not so the women, the weeping, who wail,
And I alone, again and always, shall grieve.

In Utgard-Loki's Hall

Then traveled Thor to the giants' far tracts:
    Mjollnir's master, most mighty in mettle;
Loki came with him, clever and keen-eyed
    Quickest to action, questioning always.
Also his servant, swift-footed Thialfi
    Sure as the sunrise, trustworthy as time.
Challenges offered: of racing, of wrestling,
    Imbibing and eating; they bragged they were best.

First came the feasting; Loki lunged for
    the trough; tried tireless to empty it,
But failed from the start. The trencher was
    truncated, bone and bark bolted,
Logi the champion clearly was called;
    the giants grew jovial, enjoying the games.
Wolf's-Father was wroth, felt wronged
    and offended; his ire was immense, but
The wrangle was won; fuming and
    frowning, he forced back his fury.

Then raced Thialfi against his raw rival;
    Hugi's steps hasted sharply, hurried along.
Outspeeding the other, the ogre
    pulled past him; three times the race ran,
Swifter than sky-candle
    draws dawn from the darkness.
Subdued was the servant,
    now chastened and cowed.

Impatient, the Jotuns jeered at Thor's joust,
    brought forth the biggest bug-chaser of all
Silk-tailed slinker, claws like steel scythes:
    Eyes of old emerald, coat grey and grim.

Fate favored the flame-bearded, in fury
        Frenzied; wrestled he then with worry and woe.
Beast bare budging, as bright fire flickered,
        Strained so to lift it, struggling sore.
Withal would its paws, padding and
        playing, not lift from the level, nor leave go the floor.
Ever did mouse-murderer purr all the merrier.
        Finally, one foot failed, lifting up faintly;
At cat's cost, he faltered, let fall the feline:
        Huffing, Hlorriþi now sullen and scorned.

Of drinking, he drained the draught
        Three times most deeply; barely the brew
Slipped low past the lip;
        Of wrestling, an elderly ettin-wife held him;
Bore him to the bottom, his knee hitting
        stone. However he strove, he hardly could stir
her; her hands held him captive,
        Kept him from the coup.

Then did their host hurry them homewards;
        Out to the hall's gate he escorted them.
Sternly and sober, the Jotuns' sovereign
        Bade them to return to the border remote.
As they were leaving, he let slip the lies;
        lax, senses lulled, they saw not the tricks.
No foolish feaster, howsoever hungry
        could chomp his fare faster than fire.
Thialfi raced Thought, swifter than steeds;
        from shore to shore in the squint of an eye.
Cat 'twas the world-circler, writhing and
        wily; too heavy to heft, too huge to heave.
Horn had its heel buried deep in the brine;
        Old Age was the ancient whose grasp he had grappled;
No man and no maid may master her

>   hold. All eyes imposed on by evil illusion.
> Then the Thunderer hoisted his hammer;
>   Hurled it hastily, but struck too slow.
> The giant-king, Jotuns, and hall all had
>   vanished, and vanquished, the company headed for home.

Answers (Ansuz)

You speak.
I listen.
Even when I don't like what You have to tell me,
I know that You say it not from malice,
        or boredom,
        or cruel whimsy,
        or anger,
But because these are things
    I need to hear,
    I need to absorb,
    I need to learn.
Your words are wisdom,
and even if I don't understand them now,
I will someday:
    when the time is right,
    when I need to understand them,
    when You will it.
I can kick and scream and cover my ears with my hands,
but such childish defiance
does not shut out Your words,
because I hear them not with my ears,
but with my heart,
and no matter how much I may rail
against what You have to tell me now,
eventually I will come to see
that You were right,
as You always are.

Therefore, I pray that You will understand
that I may not want to hear what You say,
Not through a rejection of Your advice to me,
    but from fear,
    from ignorance.

from despair,
and from the innocent unknowing
of the child I know myself to be
in comparison with the knowledge You have learned over vast centuries.

Understand why I shy away from You sometimes—
painful words,
and forgive me,
For You will know I will come around in time,
as I always do,
as I always have done.

And thank You for the gift of Your wisdom,
for valuing me enough to want to teach me at all,
for wanting to make me a better person.

Knowing that You find me worthy of such things
will eventually allow me to accept
that belief of, and in, myself
that I have never known.

I will strive always to never make You doubt my worth,
or regret sharing that gift with me.

And let Your words ever come unto me.

Gebo

A gift for a gift: that is the oldest law,
The most primal compact between us and Them,
and this is the law that all interaction between us
is predicated on:
Not always a tangible gift, that oldest of presents,
but respect—
For how can you honor a being, revere Them, obey Them,
Heed Their demands, do Their bidding,
without that most primal of offerings?

Generosity, hospitality: these things are bred into us,
Deeper than flesh, deeper than bone, all the way down to the soul;
Do not all men understand that,
by turning away travelers, you may—without knowing—
spurn gods in disguise?
How cursed the man who slams his door
in the face of those in need!
As They who made us gave us many gifts,
so too do They expect us to emulate Their behavior,
and give likewise to those they meet,
whether friend or stranger.
We speak of considering our tribe before all others,
and this is wise,
but how wise is it to turn your face aside
upon seeing one who might well starve to death in the road
but for the tiniest of charities that you might extend
and choose not to, because you know not his name or face?
So too does such generosity
win a man renown
for following the way of the gods,
and giving gifts even where none might be extended in return.
It is truly a man who is wealthy beyond imagining—
not in gold, but in heart—

that opens his doors and his arms to those in want.

But this generosity should not become folly:
if a man should return your hospitality with strife,
breaking frith,
exchanging truth for lies,
then he has forsaken the right to expect such gifts
from you in the future,
and even the gods would understand,
why you withhold that grace from one who has wronged you;
we are not, after all, those that turn the other cheek.

In the end, when we pass from this world,
we take nothing with us: not gold, not silver,
not cattle or corn, not swine nor sword,
not garments of silk or the meanest rags.
All that remains of a man that is tangible stays behind
when he dies—as does that one intangible thing, that,
divided, endures here and yet follows him to the Halls of the Gods:
his name and his reputation.
Good to be known as skilled with a weapon,
good also to be known as skilled with words,
but perhaps best it is to be known as
skilled with gifts—the giving, and the accepting of them,
and that name will travel with you
where no mortal wealth may go.
Therefore, let your repute be fine,
finer than costly array or gleaming gems,
and the Gods will welcome you to Their halls
while those of lesser character must be content
with tattered raiment, scraps of old bread,
and an empty mead-cup of cold, dull lead.

A gift for a gift: let your gifts
be worthy of your name,

and your name
be worthy of such gifts
as even the Gods themselves
would be proud to accept.

Hagalaz

Hail comes in many forms:
    Five-car pile-up
    Swine flu at a wedding
    Food poisoning
    Tornado
    Flash flood
    Mine collapse
    Wildfire.

Some think that the ancestors meant hail and hail alone,
perhaps because they lived in the northlands,
but we know better.

What makes so many believe this planet belongs to us?
At best, we're only borrowing it for a very little while,
And the gods know it.
Sooner or later, Nerthus will flick us off her back
and that will be the end of us.

Do not think that our demise will necessarily come about
from something great like comets, earthquakes, or hurricanes;
Bacteria can kill, too,
as every victim of bubonic plague
        cholera
        Spanish flu
        malaria
and syphilis found out.

Nor are we content to settle for those old diehards, no:
We tinker.
We improve things.
We make things work better.
We have always helped, at least a little, to weave our own destruction:

Jord and Nerthus know this,
and Skuld knows it, too.
After all, we're so good at meddling.

Hail is disruption, devastation, destruction from things
outside our control.
Whether it strikes us down one at a time or in the millions,
it has its way
and it is purest folly to think we can engineer the end
of these natural disorders which periodically wreak havoc among us.
Nor is hail restricted to only we humans;
more arrogance there, to think so.

How many trees burn in every forest fire?
How many animals drown when the rain will not cease
and the rivers overflow their banks and the dams burst asunder?

No, we cannot prevent it when things come crashing down
around our heads;
all we can do is hold on,
    try to survive,
    try to contain our shock,
    and then rebuild when the dust has settled.

Those things that bring our world down upon our heads
can make us stronger, if we let them;
can teach us important lessons, if we listen.

That does not mean it will not hurt.

When a child breaks a leg, it hurts,
and then hurts again as it heals;
but it **will** heal.
Hail teaches us to learn from pain and devastation,
and that is why it is important.

Hail is that dark and cold contrast
to the joy and light we seek in life,
and that contrast teaches us how precious joy and life truly are.

We might not appreciate the beauty of a rose
if we were not wary of its thorns;
We might not love our family so much if
we did not realize how suddenly they could be torn from us;
We might not marvel at the delight of a perfect sunny day
were there not clouds and fog and snow to show us the difference.

We might hate hail, but it is a necessary part of existence.

No light without darkness.
No day without night.
No summer without winter.

No fertility without barrenness.
No harvest without blight.
No feast without famine.

No love without hatred.
No bliss without misery.
No life without death.

Hail is the other half of the balance,
and there **must** be the balance.

Hail Hagalaz!

Isa

This stillness, this cold:
This is the oldest thing.
Before everything—
before Aes, before Van,
before man, before wight,
before jotun, before troll,
before Alf, before all—
there was only the ice.

That still point, that cold point:
that was the wheel on which the creation
of all that came after, turned—
not a potter's wheel, not a wagon wheel,
but the brilliant, icy sparkling wheel of stars
that did not yet exist,
spinning in the void of space
that also did not yet exist.
There was only the cold,
the emptiness—
and it was still.

Scientists say that space is not a void,
and is not still:
that in the vast gulfs of emptiness between the stars,
there is yet matter that we don't see:
uncountable numbers of molecules—
gases, dust, plasma, ions
—all whirling in an enormous cosmic dance
that began at the beginning, that big bang that began it all,
and has yet to end
and yet:
before all that, before that bang,
there was nothing:

a void,
>   empty and vast
>   empty and cold
>   empty and still
and only when that bang came
did the universe dance itself out of the cold
and into being.

May not poison and sparks, whirling together across
the endless void, birthing something
that had never before existed,
make a loud bang?

May not a cow's hoof, struck against the ice,
make a very loud bang?

May not the very universe itself
herald the birth of Three Mightier than all others
with the loudest bang of all?

So much of that bygone past
is lost to us now,
but parts—here, and there—lay waiting,
yet to be discovered,
>   trapped in glacial crevasse,
>   frozen within underground stream,
>   buried by ancient avalanche.
For ice preserves, as well,
holding all things uncorrupted and undiscovered
within its frozen grasp.
If the time is not yet right
(or ripe)
for those ancient secrets to be found,
then they will wait
until the ice itself wills them

to be released.

And in that moment, that lost and frozen moment,
the wheel exists, turning yet unturning
(like the particle that exists, moving yet unmoving)
its crystalline spokes extending outward to penetrate all that is,
an exquisite beauty that is everywhere and nowhere all at once,
that stillness like the hush of snow,
that emptiness like the sleep of winter,
and those radiant arms all too, too like
the arms of a snowflake, caught on the cusp
between melting and being.

Naudhiz

Adversity forces you to grow even when you don't intend to:
Grow like the dark-needled tree
    clinging to the edge of the highest precipice;
Grow like the lichen,
    clinging to the coldest rocks;
Grow like the mezereon,
    blooming pink as the dawn before the snows have even melted.
Grow into the shape that is best for your soul.
Let the storms of December and the icy winds of January
strip away those bits of your life that are unnecessary
    that distract
    that hurt
    that anger
    that waste your time and spoil your heart.
Grow—by choice, or through hardship—
Needing the sharp, swift snap of circumstance
    (boughs breaking under winter's winds)
    to reveal to yourself
Those things you rely on
    which hamper and constrain you,
    which make you small
    which make you old before your time
    even when you don't realize it.
Be not afraid to stretch out your branches
    and put down roots:
Those things that truly serve you
    will remain, untouched by pain
        or laziness, or fear,
        or rage, or the greedy demands of others.
Glory in your strength, your beauty,
    once you have found the true shape of your soul.

And then reach for the sun which is your due.

Ireland and the Celtic Lands

Red Flame

Red flame, white fire,
And I know that she is with me, always.
In the warmth of an embrace that is not seen,
In the softness of whispered words heard only by the soul's ear,
In the bright spark of her inspiration, shaping words to song.

Brigid, guiding my steps;
Brigid, showing the way;
Brigid, watching over all.

Hand that strengthens the smith's grasp;
Smile that heals the sick;
Voice that rings with the flash of the muse's gift.

Lady, three-in-one,
Gentle and mild,
Be with me, fearless, and
Guard over me when I fear;
Be with me, unraging, and
Calm my temper when fury strikes;
Be with me, sweet calm one, and
Comfort me those dark nights
When sorrow comes.

Song to Brigid at Imbolc

The hammer swings, the anvil rings
At breaking of the dawn's first light.
Like hallowed bell or solemn knell
To sweep away the winter's night.

The flames that shine in bright smith's shrine
Have burned a thousand years or more,
Undimmed by woes or rage from those
Who bring on famine, plague, or war.

They ever burn for those who yearn
For healing, skill of hands, or art,
We turn to Her whose mercies blur
The pain that burdens every heart.

As gift to She who inspires me,
I offer now my humble song,
These words of praise ring through my days,
And make the bond between us strong.

If these words meet approval sweet
From her, I have achieved my aim;
I am no bard, but labor hard
That each verse sings her holy name.

Washerwoman

Scald-crow queen,
scarlet-eyed,
you sit at the river's edge with your
hands full of bloody laundry.
Patient,
for so many men come to you
in their time.
Battle-bright, with your
sword-steel wingspan,
they fall easily to spear, spells,
And the sharp scything grip
of your talons.

Boldly,
you stride amongst the wounded.
Boldly,
you dine on death.
Boldly,
you winnow weak and strong alike.

Cuchulainn's bane,
terror of the night,
Dark Lady,
who is there who can stand in your way,
and end the ringing clash of steel,
silence the screams of the maimed,
and wash away the blood?

Advice

Just because the Phantom Queen's hand may be
gloved in blood past the elbow
Doesn't mean you shouldn't shake it, if she offers;
She's the honest sort, brutally so,
With no need for deceptions, theft, or lies.

Whether you draw back your hand whole and unscathed
or a gory stump,
The fingers (when you find them at last)
Will still bear all the rings they did before you met her
(And anyway, it's rude to refuse,
and you know how much value their kind puts on good manners).

Though she might bear many roles—
     —warrior, prophet, bestower of kingship—
go by more than one name (or shape),
Still, she's not two-faced;
The honesty in those red, red eyes might kill,
But the blade will end up in your heart,
not buried in your back.

Don't scorn her greeting, if it comes, or her aid;
Cuchulainn did that thrice,
and look at how that ended for him.
You are no Lugh's son, no legend,
and however much pride you might have for yourself,
It isn't wise to piss off a goddess
who already knows how you will die
before she's ever met you.

Don't give her a reason to wash your clothes in the stream;
Instead, speak plainly and kindly,
Tell no lies,

offer no insults or bargains,
never beg,
and you might walk away from the meeting
with both your eyes still in their sockets.
Ay, now that's a story to tell your grandchildren,
should you live long enough to have any.

You Will Know Me

As strength:
>Again and again you raise your weapon,
Fingers gripping tight to the hilt of your saber,
feeling the heaviness of steel as you ready it once more,
feeling the burn in shoulders and back and arms
as you bring it down repeatedly, teeth gritted,
slashing through flesh, hacking through bone,
understanding that the span of your life may be
measured in the number of times you can lift it up again.

As courage:
>It takes nerve to bolt up over the top of your fortification,
screaming profanities at the foe as you race toward the
oncoming bullets. Your weapon you tossed aside before you rose,
rushing toward certain death to scoop up one of your own,
one fallen, hurt too badly to move himself, a friend you refuse
to abandon to his certain end, risking your own death just to
ensure
that, when he passes, it will be among friends,
 and not face-down and alone in the mud and the blood.

As fear:
>Only the dead and the mad know no terror, do not feel the
quickened rush of breath in their lungs as they wait for the
yellow-green gas to come creeping through the claustrophobic
rabbit-warrens of the trenches. Those who fear know a single
will render their insides to jelly, and can feel the hurried
thump-thump of their heart as it frenzies with the hope that a
kinder death than the one that makes one cough out their
own insides is the one that will greet them this day.

As rage:
>Watching one friend after another get cut down,

dodging each hail of bullets as they speed through the air
like a swarm of angry bees, but whose stingers bring
death instead of just a little pain. You see the shattered faces
of those who met their end at the hands of smiling, laughing
children whose hands reached out not for hugs or sweets,
but to thrust live hand grenades at you, even knowing they
would meet their own end from the handful of green metal.
So many lost for so little, and senseless suffering all around.

As pain:

Under the dull gray-green of the medical tent's roof,
you lay near death, feeling the throbbing agony where
the foot you once had used to be. That phantom sensation
is no less real for all that no foot remains attached to that leg,
nor any flesh whole past the knee. The cannon's ball did its job
all too well, and you draw another tortured breath, listening
as the medics make their way down the line of injured,
listening to the screams as maimed and mangled limbs are
removed, cauterized with a torch, painted with tar. The
doctors are close now, and you lay there with fists clenched,
waiting for your turn with blade and fire, uncertain as to
whether it would be better for the doctors to come before
the last dregs of your life bleed out through shattered bone
and ruined flesh.

As loss:

You can count the numbers of your fallen friends,
but it takes more than the sum of your fingers and toes,
or even those of the few brothers-in-arms that still remain.
You have become well-acquainted with Me, watching as
the carrion-birds strut the field after the battle's end,
feasting richly on the remains of those from both sides,
growing fat as they gorge themselves on eyes and entrails.
You miss those who have gone before you; miss the
camaraderie you shared with those you bonded with,

knowing that nothing bonds people together more surely
than facing death, not knowing which of you will fall
and whom will remain behind to mourn those who
have already gone on that final journey without you.

As despair:
When you are confronted with the fact that you are
fighting and dying for things of no importance, of things
that will never change, for causes that have been fought
over again and again for centuries, there comes a moment
when you realize that you are spending your life, the lives
of your fellow soldiers, the lives of the foe, for no
reason worth expending the effort—not even to spit at
those who sent you here to die. Then it sinks in, that utter
lack of hope, and whether you sit in the dark of night
waiting for the blast that will bring it all to an end,
or whether you wait under the blazing eye of day,
helpless against the forces that have brought you here,
you abandon any expectation that you might get out
of this hell with flesh and soul and mind unscathed.

As madness:
War is Hell, they say, and amidst the carnage and death
there are those who survive even when they wish they had not;
broken in body, but more broken in mind, reliving every close
call, every explosion, every friend falling dead before their eyes.
Those who have gone through this horror and come out the
other side carry that Hell inside them always, flinching at every
slammed door, every car that backfires, every crash of thunder.
Some learn to live with that Hell, embrace it, accept it; others
end up giving in to its whispers, taking up arms once again,
recreating the battles where they did not die, and felling innocents
they imagine as enemies, until they are finally brought down
by those who must oppose them, and are delivered at last
into the shelter of the silent peace they sought—

the peace that only I can bring them.

As numbness:
> How many deaths can one see before it ceases to bring grief; how many stones can be piled upon one's soul before that soul is crushed underneath the weight of that pain? In the roar and crash of battle, amid the sweep of rifle fire, only so much can be registered, can be felt, before even the prospect of one's own end no longer brings fear, only unfeeling indifference, and finally longing: an end to strength and courage, fear and rage, loss and madness, pain and despair. All such burdens leave scars, inside and out, and their final sum is the wish for unending peace: of one sort, or another.

I am War, and Death during War, and all War's horrors.

As strength, as courage, as fear,
As rage, as pain, as loss,
As despair, as madness, as numbness:

You *will* know Me.

Keening

Among us, it is well known:
thwarting the Great Queen is not wise.
refusing her, even less so.

My son refused her thrice.
bold, he was;
strong, he was.
the wisest man in all Ireland, though—
none could claim that of him.

A woman wants what a woman wants;
when She was taken with love for him,
her heart wanted only its due;
I do not think when She cursed him,
She recalled that he was my son.
There is no feud laying between us
due to his death by Her will.

Hear now my lament for my son,
O sons and daughters of Eire!
My son was Cuchulainn the Brave.
Cuchulainn the Bold,
Cuchulainn the Most Skilled of Many Warriors!
As a child, he wrestled and slew
the great hound of Culainn,
then vowed to take its place,
guarding the hall of Culainn.
In battle, he stood against many,
striking down his foes with his great spear,
the spear of many barbs.
He bested the warrior woman Aife,
then fathered on her the warrior Conlaoch;
she wove the destiny for both,

demanding three things from her son,
and thereby ensured his death at the hands of his father.
On the field of battle, he slew his childhood friend,
in honor unable to let his friend's challenge pass untested.

But that night, that night he heard the loud cry from the North,
my son, my son the hound of battle,
He wove his own doom, turning aside
the love of the daughter of the King,
finding no time for a woman's caresses
when there was battle to be had.
and so he refused her once.
She insisted she would aid him in battle with her skills,
and he told her he had no need of a woman's aid,
and so he refused her twice.
Her desire turned to anger, and then she warned him:
if he would have neither her love nor her aid,
then he would have her wrath.
He responded that he did not fear any woman's hatred,
and so he refused her thrice.
He drew his sword to attack her, and
then it was that she showed herself for whom she was,
the gore-crow of battle sitting on the skeleton branch of a tree,
And even then, he did not fear.

His three refusals led to three wounds;
his three wounds led him to wound her thrice,
and those three wounds led to three healings.
At last the day came,
the day of his death,
and three crones there were,
offering hospitality such as he could not refuse,
ere he were to break his geas against such,
but the meat they cooked was dog,
the flesh of a hound like Culain's hound he had slain,

and in eating the food they offered,
he broke that geas,
and so brought his doom upon himself.

Ochone! Ochone, for my son is dead!
Ochone! Ochone, for the man best at battle in all the world
has fallen to rash words and pride.
Ochone! Ochone! Let the world mourn,
for a man can never be but what he is,
though it mean his death.
Ochone! Ochone! Hear me, people of all the land of Eire!
Hear me, descendants of all the folk!
I am Lugh, satirist, warrior, harper, and king,
and today I mourn for my son!
Heed my words as I cry, Ochone!
Though his life was short, his legend shall be long,
and lay over all the world throughout the ages of man.
Ochone! Ochone! Ochone!
Cuchulainn, the hound of Culainn,
that once was the boy Setanta,
my son, the mighty, has fallen!
Ochone!

Kingly

The enemy saw my girth,
my rude way of dressing,
my cheerful nature,
and branded me a fool.
They were wrong, of course;
they thought to weaken me,
humiliate me with their demands:
As if eating a huge bowl of porridge
would leave me unfit for battle!
They learned, to their grief,
how wrong they were,
when I slew Cirb, son of Buan,
when he entered the fray.

Some among my own thought me simple;
they forgot my deeds of strategy
at the Plain of Props, and thought
they could trick me into giving up
such things as were mine;
when my most beautiful son
sought a place of his own, and
my half-brother,
the most skilled one of us all,
thought to help him, they could come up
with no more than a petty play on words,
and that in our own tongue;
yet they thought that enough to take
the Bru na Boinne, and I let them,
for I love my son, and am I not
the most amiable and easy-going
of all of our folk?

Some among the bards think me
indolent, and lazy, and slow,
content to let others do my work for me,
as when I handed command of our forces
to my half-brother during the heated battle,
as when I might have served as champion
to our silver-handed king, but left that task
to my brother; but I had other matters to
contemplate and carry out, and those things
required more of me than a moment's stolen grace.

Some thought me weak and cowardly;
those who were thus mistaken are all dead.
Skulls smashed in battle, brains spilled,
blood loosed in rivers from the veins where it swam.
I suffer none to hold me in such contempt,
and showed my foes the errors of their ways.
None may stand against my mighty club,
nor the heft of the thews that wield it,
nor the strength of the one who lifts it.

Some account me lusty, and on this,
they are correct, though mistaken are those
who think I show disrespect for my wife
by my trysts with others;
but when was it a crime for a man or a god
to admire a beautiful face, a shapely form,
and want to explore such beauty further?
If such is a crime, then all of us are criminals,
and not just men, but women too, though
many would not care to admit to such.
But I refuse to recoil from such joy and pleasure
when the opportunities present themselves,
and of me and my prowess, no woman I've
bedded has ever complained.

Even the Phantom Queen Herself,
fierce and dreadful and terrifying to behold,
has known the embrace of my arms,
the skill with which I wield that other club of mine,
and when we were finished, She lamented not.
And in this, I am content.

Those who might mock me, think to cheat me,
hold me in disdain, find me unwitting, beware:
Among all the Tuatha De, you will find no greater King.
Underestimate me at your peril.

Etain's Lesson

I endured.

Target of a madwoman's jealousy and hatred
simply for existing, for loving and being loved,
I endured.

What more shall I say of it?

I was born blessed to be beautiful, but beauty can be a curse:
Few looked beyond the charms of my face and form
to learn more of what lay beneath—
but *he* did.

The man I was fated to wed, to love and lose,
knew me for more than my beauty:
He saw my deft hand with harp and spindle,
how I loved to sing,
The way I sat a horse to the hunt,
the tears I wept when I saw illness and poverty,
sorrow and death;
the way I hurt when those my father ruled also hurt—
He saw to the heart of me, and loved me for it.

And shall I speak of him, my king, my love?
I would have loved him had he been the poorest shepherd,
or a blind beggar at the side of the road.

Oh, but he was a fine King, and no mistake—
his lean and powerful frame,
his prowess in battle,
the way he dispensed justice and mercy alike
among his subjects,
but these things would have been part of him—

his bravery, his kindness, the delight of his shine and shape
(and yes, I admit the irony in admiring his beauty
all the while I disdain those who only desire me for my own)—
even if he had never made the voice of the Lia Fail ring in recognition.

So there we were: two souls united in love.

And then there was Fuamnach.

If a viper could wear the form of a woman,
and kill with a venomed kiss, it would be Fuamnach.
If malice and envy and rage could put on two legs
and walk among men, it would be Fuamnach.
If magic could curdle a heart until it swelled, burst open
like a rotten egg, and birth a monster, it would be Fuamnach.

Oh, she was beautiful, of that there was no doubting:
hair the hue of the sky at midnight at new moon, and
eyes like gleaming gems, hard and cold.
And none could doubt her skills with sorcery.

But those two things were all she had to recommend her,
and my Midir put her aside.

Her rage was as boundless as the great surge of waters that
birthed the world, and as deep:

She waited little time to exact her revenge, using her spells
to dwindle and diminish me as the blessed Spring sunlight
diminishes an icicle,
And one day when Midir was away,
then I, like that icicle, melted,
Becoming no more than a small pool of water on the surface
of the fertile earth of my garden.
But, like tears, like the ocean's brine,

the water I had become—
(still living, feeling, thinking, fearing,
in pain and confusion and terror)
—drained into the soil, melting and merging with a
clutch of worm's eggs there,
Until I hatched from one as a worm.

What woe then!

My senses restored, I could see what I had become,
feel the slime that sheathed my form,
hear the thrashings and mindless chewing of the other worms
I shared the soil with,
and I turned myself upward, wiggled and writhed through
the dirt around me,
And thrust up through the surface
to the clean air and bright sun above.

But the bright sun burned my soft and weak flesh
as it never had before,
And through the clean air dove a bird, swooping down to take its meal,
its sharp cry the only warning I got
—or needed—
and I dove down into the dirt again.

For seven years, I endured beneath the soil,
eating of the rotting things that worms must eat,
and making more soil from it.

For seven years, I moved ceaselessly, evading
the attention of amorous worms, never resting,
never sleeping.

For seven years, I wept without surcease,
mourning my Midir as if he were dead to me,

and wondering if he thought me dead as well.

And then the day came that fire burned through me,
a physical pain greater than any I had ever before felt,
and I raced for the surface of the soil,
praying for cool water to quench those inner flames,
for rain or snow or even the soothing balm of autumnal mist.
Instead, I broke free of the ground in the midst of a spring evening,
and the gardens were beaded with dew.

I thrashed there on the grass, rolling and rolling,
and little by little, the soft, gelatinous flesh of the worm shape
I wore began to slough away,
And I felt damp, broad, delicate petals unfold from my back.
As they dried, they blocked out the sun;
What light filtered through them fell, stained, broken,
the color of violets raining around me like a halo.

No longer lacking legs, but having sprouted six;
No longer ears, but antennae;
No longer two eyes, but a hundred diamond lenses to peer through,
And I spread my wings and soared into the air
to embrace the sun
before leaving the garden to search for my Midir.

I found him in his hall, alone, grayed by melancholy,
and came to rest on his shoulder.
He looked up, startled, and a tired smile passed over his face—
the first, I knew somehow, in a long while.

It was not the same as our marriage—
how could it be?
I could not hold him, nor be held by him;
could not kiss him, nor be kissed by him;
could not croon his name, nor did he know 'twas me,

to do the same.
But where he went, I went;
when he slept, I slept atop his bedstead;
and when he ate, he fed me honey and the nectar of flowers,
and it was enough: I was content.

So of course it could not last.

Like a child enjoying a toy only to have it snatched away,
our renewal was all the more sweet for being so brief:
just a year we were reunited;
and the pain and grief all the greater for that sweetness;
When a mighty wind came blasting out of the North,
hurling me from him,
I feared I would die.
For seven long years, I was blown about by the wind,
my wings in tatters, no place to rest but the rocks of the sea,
and I despaired
Until another of the folk, mighty Dagda's fair son,
found me, caught me between his nimbly-cupped hands, and—
at war with my Midir, unable to return me to him,
—but not so dishonorable as to slay me to hurt my lover—
and not able to stop long on his way,
built me a tiny house of wood and stone to shelter me from the blast.
And there, under his watchful eye,
I rested for many and many a year,
Separated from my beloved, but safe.

Yet one day, when Aengus' attention was elsewhere
(though only for a moment),
the winds rose again, shattering my shelter,
and hurling me across the wide world once more.

O the gales! O the blasts!

The winds whipped 'round, year after year,
tearing my wings to bits, and finally blowing me through a window
into the hall of Étar, where I fell into his lady wife's wine-cup.
and was swallowed.

I endured.

Nine months' sleep I slept, and in that sleep,
I changed my form once more,
shedding wings and legs and many-jeweled eyes
like a snake sheds its skin,
shifting my shape until a daughter was born to Étar and his lady.

And did I remember my fair lord Midir, as I grew?

I did not, for birth wipes away all memories of the past,
drawing a veil over our eyes akin to that of death, and—
bearing my own name through a pretty coincidence,
I thrived, gained grace of form,
skill of hands, and beauty.
And when I came of age,
I was wed to King Eochaid, a goodly man.

And that is when my lord and love Midir found me.

I worried when Eochaid's brother Ailill grew ill in Eochaid's absence,
and wept when I realized it was for love of me;
yet I could not let my husband's dear brother die, no matter the
shame I would bring upon myself; I vowed to do what I must
to restore him. And thus I made arrangements to meet him in a tryst,
and went, cloaked in night's darkness, to a shadowed wood to meet
   him;
the man I met wore the face of Ailill, spoke with his voice,
yet I knew somehow that this was not Ailill,
and I turned from him and fled.

Three times I met with him,
and three times I sensed that the one I faced
was not the brother of my husband,
but some stranger using magic
to ape his form. And so two times,
I forebore, returning to my home with
my honor unstained.

And the third time we met, he revealed who he really was:
my Midir, my lord and my love, and I his wife and beloved before
foul sorcery parted us.
And yet, though I could see he spoke the truth,
I could not break my vows
to Eochaid; I told him as much,
and that I would not go away with him
save if Eochaid himself gave permission,
which I knew would never happen.
His grief and loss painted themselves over his face like rain,
and I turned aside, that third time, and returned to my wedding bed.

You know the rest—the games of fidchell he lost, the vast wagers
he paid, the tasks set, and at last, the game he won;
the price he demanded as his prize,
the lengths Eochaid went to—
(a goodly man, but not my Midir)
—to keep me in his possession.

All for naught.

One kiss, and the veil over my old memories rent like decayed lace;
One kiss, and I threw my white arms 'round him and sobbed in joy;
One kiss, and we became swans, rising through the King's roof
to fly away to Bri Leith.

Eochaid pursued, of course; what man worthy of that name would not?

His men sought to tear down the mound;
years they dug, with their shovels and their picks—
a score of years, in which I aged not, faded not.
At last, Midir gave him a choice:
Could he choose me correctly from a crowd of maidens,
I would be his.

Eochaid agreed, and fifty girls
beautiful as a new-budded rose were brought forth.
And he chose.

And he chose wrong.

He did not simply choose incorrectly, did Eochaid;
he chose **wrong**.

Wrong, for it was his own daughter,
birthed from my body in that score of years,
fair of face and like of mien to me,
that he chose, and took home, and bedded.

Not until she birthed a child of her own did she tell him,
for not until that moment, when the swaddled babe was
pressed into her arms, did the veil Midir had thrown over
her own memories lift.

They say I never loved Eochaid, or how could I have left him?

They say I never loved Eochaid, or how could I have given him
his own daughter to wife?

They say I never loved Eochaid, but it was out of love that I gave him
the greatest gift I could: the only woman ever born to equal my beauty,

which was—in the end—all he cared about.

For he was no Midir.

What he gave to me, I gave back to him, a gift for a gift,
as is just and proper and right; that I would be diminished by
giving the gift meant nothing, for giving any gift means
we pay a cost: in time, in materials, in effort, in gold, in love.
And so it was here; for was she not flesh of my flesh, child of my body,
and beloved, as well?

Those who read this may recoil in horror at the thought:
that I gave up my daughter to her father's bed.
And indeed, the tales tell that her father was horrified,
that she too was grieved; yet the tales are wrong, spun by liars,
long after those who still followed the old ways had passed, for
things were different in those days, and are not those of
the Sidhe perfect in form and health, unable to bear monsters?
Did not the Dagda, beget of Danu,
sleep with his own mother to
sire Ogma? True that, and equally true
that Brigid, daughter of the Dagda,
was wedded to Tuireann, Ogma's son, her father's grandson.
And many more besides; and all of a kind.
I tell you this: my daughter was content with her husband,
as I was content with my Midir, my love and my lord,
and content also when the Mac Og brought Fuamnach's head
to the house, for then I knew that we should never be parted again.

And so it was. For I endured.

This is what I say to you. This is the lesson I share.
This is my offering, spun out across the ages to all who suffer:
No pain is eternal.
No situation is hopeless.

Nothing is forever.
When it seems there is nothing left,
When it seems as though there is no one left that cares,
When it seems as though all you know and love is gone,
Think again.
And endure.
Endure.
Endure.

Long-Armed, Many-Skilled

No man who had come to the doors
of the High King's hall
before that day had gained entrance
without displaying their mastery of
a single unique skill;
in that way, it was something of a
first-come, first-served position;
to demonstrate before the court and all its lords
that your talents in a given field
rose supreme over all others was
a great honor indeed, and to be accepted
into that hall to sit among those noble peers
was a greater honor still.

He came to the door
of Tara's hall barely a man,
much like the son
he would someday foster;
the gatekeeper asked him
to demonstrate the skill
that would gain him entrance,
but for every skill the young man
asked to demonstrate, the answer
came back always that
there was already one within, sheltered
under that fair hall's roof,
who could perform such deeds.
Smith, bard, champion, wright,
harpist, poet, crafter, swordsman:
all dwelt within the hall, leaving no room
for any pups standing outside in the cold
to challenge them for their spot.

And did he despair? Did he admit defeat,
let broad shoulders sag, his long spear-throwing
hands fall useless to his side,
only to turn and walk away?
Of course not; such is not the stuff
that legends are made of.
Instead, he flashed a wry and cocky grin,
eyes flashing, the light from the hearth
inside the hall casting radiance in a halo
'round his fair-browed head,
and challenged the gatekeeper:
So many fine men, with so many fine talents…
but is there one under your roof
who can boast of having mastered
all such skills?

And of course, the gatekeeper could not answer,
Yes, it is thus. The lad found the look on the man's face
comical, and in no time, he was
ushered into the presence of Nuada, High King,
and was commanded to demonstrate the talent and skill
of his hands; whereby he agreed and hurled the
largest flagstone under that spacious roof from
one end of the hall to the other.

Then it was time for praise, for boasting, for feasting,
for fine drink, fair-browed women, laughter, and joy.
Little did the lad know of the shadow that hung heavy
over that hall; less did he know that soon,
he would sit the seat of the High King himself.
But that is a tale for another night.

On this night, as we do on the night when
the death of the lad's foster mother's death
was commemorated,

we sing of Lugh Lamfada, Lugh Samildanach,
drink a toast to that valiant hero and mighty god
who has never died, nor ever will.
Though men who worship lies, or nothing at all,
may claim he is only a children's story,
those who have heard the voice of the Long-Armed,
the Many-Skilled, know well that no child's tale
is worthy of the adoration, respect, and love that we
bear for him.
Hail Lugh! May your name continue to be
sung down the ages for a thousand-thousand generations.

Feral

Treasure knows no laws.

Man understands this; greed as a force of corruption
stands without equal.
For the glitter of gold,
for the shine of silver,
for the call of copper,
A man will sell his mother,
a maid slaughter her lover,
a mother cast away her child.
Neither druids nor bards are immune to the laws of such spoils,
Nor are gods.

It hurt when the beast took my arm. Not at once;
My heart blazed with the flames of battle,
and I roared as I closed with him,
No more aware that my sword-hand lay on the grass,
still clasping my blade,
The rim of my shield laying nearby,
Than swine are aware that they fill their bellies in summer
Only to fall before the butcher's blade come autumn.
They say that I cried out for aid; I have no memory of this,
Though I doubt not the honorable word of my honorable friends.
My companions rushed in to fill the gap between myself and my foe:
My brother from Norway was first to my side, moving to place himself
Between myself and the warrior that sought my life; fast and furious
Were the blows between Aengaba's sword and Sreng's bloodied spear.
In heartbeats, the Dagda stood shoulder-to-shoulder with Aengaba,
And this, at last, made my foe quit the field,
Unwilling to face two such heroes.
Then, and only then, did I fall; then did the Dagda
Summon kings to guard me, and doctors to staunch the bleeding,
And women of healing to bind my wounds,

And I was carried from the field, near dead.

There is no finer man of healing than Dian Cecht;
Miracles can he perform, illnesses that would kill he can
Drive away like whipped curs, but even he, so skilled,
Could not restore my arm; the blood had fled from it,
The raw meat and bone of it trampled into the muddy field
Until every sinew shattered and the skin was rent by a thousand heels.

But he gave me what he could: a hand of silver,
More finely wrought than any jewel,
the very strength and shape of my own,
Every pore, every scar, every fold of finger and gleam of muscle
Akin to my own of flesh and bone.
And so cunningly was it wrought, that only by its hue could it be told
Apart from my own.

But it was not flesh, not perfect and part of me.
Oh, aye, sealed by Creidne to the scarred shoulder
where the original had hung,
And yes, of power and might alike with that,
But the Tuatha De demand that their king
be flawless, without imperfection.
I could no longer claim such a truth,
And so I stepped aside.

Three things breed resentment in a man's heart:
Greed for the wealth he cannot have,
Longing for the respect he once held from every man,
And the fire for revenge that cannot be gained.

Many's the valorous man that fell in that battle,
Yet he who took my arm remained until the end.
He challenged me to single combat again,
before Dian Cecht had fitted me

With that arm of argent, and I bade him
bind his own sword-arm behind him.
The cur would not consent to such a compromise,
And instead of that final battle,
Wherein I might still have bested him,
The Children of Danu agreed to divide the fair lands between
Ourselves and them.

My recompense denied. No chance was I given
To strike Sreng down; the pain like poison inside my heart grew,
Festered,
Twining its cold, shining tendrils around the core of me,
And something inside
Awoke.

Three things there are that live upon this world:
The kingdom of those plants
that grow and take their strength from the sun,
The kingdom of those creatures that breathe,
and take their glory in battle,
And the kingdom of the gods,
that take pleasure from every praise given them
from the lips of man.

King no longer; perfect no longer;
I suffered in sullen silence, while the white worm of hatred
Writhed in my heart like a serpent in the haymow.
At length, I began to draw away from my fellows and my friends,
Perceiving some mockery in their slantside glances.
They say my sickness was upon me, and they did not lie;
Not the sickness within me before Dian Cecht had given to me
A hand of silver, but the sickness inside my chest,
As the three things which bred resentment did their deadly work.

The day came when my hand moved, and yet I moved it not;

The day came when my hand grasped, and yet I bade it not to grasp;
There came the day when my hand
struck out at one I had no will to strike,
A poor and humble charcoal-maker whose roof I sheltered under,
And the wretch fell down dead,
head split from crown to jaw and streaming blood
From the blow of my silver hand.
Then it was that I understood: the poison in my heart had moved
Through all the streams of my blood, and lastly reached
The scar whereunto the silver hand was grafted,
And yet despite the shield of scar between blood and bright metal,
The venom coursed throughout.
Hatred for Sreng and the fire for revenge bade my fingers curl;
Lust for the honor all the Tuatha
had once showered upon me as king—
Now bestowed upon that cruel, petty, pretty princeling Bres!—
And greed for the wealth I no longer had:
The silver like that of the hand itself;
Its shine and its weight called to my hand,
And it responded in kind:
Treasure knows no laws.

Once a god, I fell from their company and became
No better than a man; hard but hale, sturdy and sore.
Once a man, the poison flooded my veins, flowed to my hand,
And I fell again, striking down those who would aid me,
Knowing neither the nobility of the Tuatha De
Nor the decency of man; an animal I was, no more than that:
Ravening and greedy, lusting and violent,
Consuming or destroying all that crossed my path,
A feral beast needing healing—or destruction.

In my last moment of clarity, I secreted myself
away from all men, all maids;
Deep in the darkest woods of the fair isle I hid myself,

And hoped—in vain—that I would perish before another innocent
Fell beneath my unwilling blows.
But keen eyes noticed my absence:
Miach son of Dian Cecht had conceived
Of a charm that would restore my hand of flesh to me,
Confident in his own skills, finding the work of his father deficient,
And over all the land he sought for me, until finding me,
He came upon me in a slumber,
and knowing the evil of the hand of silver,
Deepened that slumber with a brew of herbs
Bestowed upon him by his sister, radiant Airmed,
And conveyed me, all unknowing, to his own shelter.

There, over three days and three nights,
He sang the charm he had created;
The first night, flesh returned to clothe the bones;
The second night, sinew and tendon grew
to weave bone and muscle to each other;
The third night, skin gleaming bright was restored over all, and he
Removed the silver hand and cast it
struggling and bloated with poison into the fire.
Then took he up the hand of flesh he had healed,
And affixed it once again to its proper place at my shoulder.
All in a daze I flexed my fingers, staring as each one moved,
The secret of my evil buried inside my heart,
Fading quickly as Airmed's balm washed away the poisons,
And once again I rose, facing the one who had made me whole,
Facing those who crowded around me,
Facing the Tuatha De who would never come to know
That the one they hailed as king once and king to come again
Had been, when all virtue and vanity and valor were torn away,
No more than a beast.

Cruinniuc's Folly

My man was a braggart, aye,
and I curse the stupid mouth which sought to gain pride
from my skill.

But I doubt that even he, dimwitted as he was,
expected these men of Ulster
to be so cruel.
They could see how far along I was,
my belly ripe and swollen as any harvest fruit,
huge and vast as the full moon
in the autumn sky.

They did not care.

Faster I was, he claimed, than even
the King's splendid horses.
Very well, the King's men said,
then have her prove it.

Only when those words came to his ears
did my man realize his foolishness;
by then, of course, it was too late.

Three things there are that even a brave man
does not wish to face:
> a dog starved of its meals,
> a river in full flood,
> and a mother protecting her children.

They loosed the horses and we ran;
ran like a ravenous bear followed close behind,
ran under the scorching glare
of the midsummer sun,

ran as if to do so was to outrun our own deaths.

With each step, my belly shook like a lake that
a giant hurled dead trees into; my insides crashed against
each other like a bag full of stones grinding meal.
The ground was soft, dry, untrustworthy;
pebbles waited to bruise a sole, to twist
a foot under, to be kicked back up from the earth
by a horse's hoof and put out an eye—or worse.

We ran the full field. Each step was a torture, and
I feared for the life inside me, my breath burning in my chest
as we reached the halfway point, neck and neck with
the fastest steed.

And then my water broke.

The first of the birthing-pangs seized my belly
and squeezed it like a giant fist, stealing the air from my lungs.
The pain was enough to stun me, stagger me,
and yet I did not quit, refused to go down.
With my gown's lower half soaked with fluids
(and no small amount of blood), I ran.

I ran with fury in my heart and venom on my lips.
I ran with ice in my veins and rage in my eyes.
I ran, and I cursed my man's slipshod mouth,
and the King's men of Ulster,
and even the life within me.

I ran. And I ran. And I ran.

The pangs quickened, because fiercer,
each one a dagger blossoming in the pit of my womb.
And I ate my own wrath, let it give me strength,

let it propel me onward even though my heart wished
only to explode in my chest,
and my belly wanted only to split wide open,
the better to spill its burden onto the ground.

I let the rage blind me, drive me,
even numb me to the agony I felt.

And I crossed the finish line ten hands'-span ahead of
the Ulster King's swiftest mount.

I dropped then, breathing hard, hiking up my filthy skirt,
the life inside me thrashing and screaming to be loosed.
Quickly, out they spilled, twins that screamed long
and lustily as they met the air outside their old cradle of flesh.

All eyes were on me as I bit and tied off their cords,
swaddled them in my torn-asunder wrap, nursed them until they slept,
and then rose to my feet:
sweating, bloody, exhausted.
Not a single man's eyes would meet my own, not even
those of my man.

As they had known no mercy, no mercy did I show them.

I let loose with my curse: because they did not let up when my time
was on me, so would they feel my pains:
the clutching, dark and bloody grunting of a woman in hard labor.
Each of them, no matter how far he fled from Ulster,
would feel the same pangs as I had,
when their greatest need was on them.
And where I let the pain drive me onward, so it would serve
to unman these cruel cowards, every one.

They stood in shocked silence as I voiced my curse,

then one by one melted away in shame, dogs with
their tails tucked betwixt their legs.
And I bore up my babes, turned my back on my man,
and left him standing there dumbly, fated to live alone forevermore.

A woman protecting her children protects also herself.
Her choices, her reasons, her heart, her line.

And woe eternal unto the man that attempts to thwart her.

Fuamnach's Accusation

When the bards tell her story,
I am always the villain:
The mold upon the bread,
The worm at the apple's heart,
The flies feasting on spoiled meat.
In all the world's ways, how is that fair?
Midir was my husband,
But all it took was one look upon her lovely face,
And he was bewitched.

Oh, yes, she *was* lovely—lovely and kind—
And indeed, that is all they ever say about her,
But beauty does not excuse all other evils.

And was I not beautiful, as well?
My hair was dark, as a well at night is dark;
My eyes were the color of violets at dusk;
No yearling fawn had so slim or sleek a form.
But she—honey-haired, dawn-eyed—
Had only to smile, and he was seduced.

Those who know the story charge me as the villain, and yet—
Do we not execute the man who steals from his master,
Whether that theft be of a loaf of bread or his weight in gold?
If warriors come to raid and take away cattle,
And are caught by the warriors of the house they steal from,
Is not the penalty for their deeds death?
She stole my husband; then, by our law,
Her head should be stricken from her body,
And displayed among all the peoples,
As a warning to those who might rob and plunder.

The tales leave out so very much;
The audience of a bard who hears this tale that he tells,
They do not understand: him I truly loved.

When he put me aside for her, I vowed:
As she had stolen my love from me, so I, with my arts,
Would steal the years of her life from her,
That she might not spend them at his side.
She made a lovely fly, the tales do not lie;
But a fly, no matter how it may delight the eyes,
Is not a woman, cannot lie with a man as a maid can.
But fate conspired to twist my enchantments;
Through its machinations, she was drank down in a cup of wine
By the wife of Etar at Inber Cichmane,
And once again born as a woman.

Then the Young Son discovered
Etain had been reborn, that she was not still
Safely in his bower at the Brugh na Boyne,
And in his rage at being deprived
Of the one he had sworn to shelter in safety,
He tracked me down, and with his blade
Struck off my head.

Surprised?
Yes, I speak to you now with only the arts
I learnt from my tutor,
And only my head remains.
It is hardly the first time that a severed head
Retained great power, and spoke, and could wield
All the arts of power; Bran spoke to his men
After his own head had been severed from his body,
And because of his wise words, it lays buried beneath
The tower of London, protecting Britain to this day
(Though that fool Arthur thought he had dug it up!)

So, too, do I speak with my arts now,
For my mind is preserved, my soul stands fast,
And though my heart may be parted from my best part,
Still I can remember my love.

There was in all of Eire no charm so great
That it could break her power over Midir;
And as the Sidhe are timeless and eternal,
It remains so to this day; to this day, they are united,
His hand holding hers, his heart slaved to hers,
And I alone under the hill of stones where Mac Og buried me.
But stone is not enough to shield them from my wrath;
Nor, had he burned me, would fire be enough to save them from my
    rage;
Even were I only ashes, still could I reach out with my hatred and
    power
And destroy them.
And I will do so.

I wait only for the most auspicious hour, between day and night,
At dusk or dawn, when neither moon nor sun shall shine in the sky,
And then I shall destroy them.

Any moment now.
Any day now.

Willingly he chooses his servitude to her,
And so I include him, my love, in her doom.

Any moment now.
Any day now.

For no man or woman or child may escape their fate.
And as I met mine, so they, too, shall find
That the love they thought they shared

Is not so strong as to protect them from the bitterness
Of a woman scorned and slain
A woman who has had centuries to plot and to plan.

Any moment now.
Any day now.

Are they prepared?
For I come, and nothing in all the world
Shall stay my hand.
I am justice, delayed but not denied,
And by the thief and by the thieved alike,
The penalty must be paid.

O my husband, o hated thief,
Weep and wail your woes to the heavens!
My time is now, and now I come.

Herne

"There is an old tale goes, that Herne the hunter,
Sometime a keeper here in Windsor forest,
Doth all the winter time at still midnight,
Walk around about an oak, with great ragg'd horns;
And there he blasts the tree, and takes the cattle;
And makes milch-kine yield blood, and shakes a chain
In a most hideous and dreadful manner."

—*The Merry Wives of Windsor*, William Shakespeare

I.
White; through the woods
you stride—
toward and away—
     leaping
     flying
     living
     dying.

Fierce heart,
Antlers a crown
     eyes like fire
     eyes like the ocean
     eyes like the moon.

Feet silver as
     the ripple of fish in the stream
Fleet one,
adored one,
majestic one:
Lover and friend.

I seek you in legend and lore:

Be with me now
    and forever.

II.
A rustle.
Nothing more, but I froze
    hearing the forest whisper
    hearing the wind pray
    hearing the hawk scream.

The loam, the rotting leaves:
My nose burned with their damp incense,
Petals speckling the moss.
Here: hoofprints—
cloven, sharp, filling slowly with water.
I knelt to drank,
closed my eyes
    listened
    tasted him
    followed.

III.
I know that I hunt the god created.
The vision not celestial but terrestrial:
Man-born.
That makes him no less real.
In my nostrils, the reek of his shaggy head:
    deer's hide
    autumn's crisp bite,
    shadows,
death.

White stag,
Antler-crowned,
Silver-hoofed.

Waiting for Samhain,
waiting for the turn of the year,
> the death of the season,
> the birth of the new year.
Be my lover and be my god, they sing:
be my lover, my lord.

IV.
You are not the only one who wears a crown of horns:
> Mithras,
> Pan,
> Ammon,
> Cernunnos.

The Christians name you devil and fear you.
I do not fear you.
Even your greatest gift—
> the end,
> the all,
> the darkness,
Is only the continuation,
> the consummation,
> > of the aging of the light,
> > the fading of the day.

White stag, white:

> I see you in the moon,
> tide in, tide out, breakers roaring,
> row of cloud's waves upon waves,.

> I see you in the snow,
> ice-glazed, knife-sharp, slippery treason,
> the crust of November's lace gone old.

I see you in the lightning-flash,
fire-pale, enraged, loud,
your voice roaring fury against the sky.

I see you in the bleached frame of barren bone:
ivory, voiceless and serene,
this, my fate, the fate of all, reduced from charnel reds
to the purity of dust.

O, hart of my heart,
Be my lover.
    ravish me
    ravage me
    savage me.
For I am savage,
Feral kin,
Fit and fitting,
    fit for you,
    fit to you,
    and fitted to you.
Engender in me
And in me be consumed.

V.
Yule, and again the wheel turns,
Dark to light,
Not day to night.
Swift, sure-footed,
Lead me, tease me, pursue me,
Past Imbolc when the Fire awakens,
Bright to your darkness,
Life to your inevitable end,
Ending, as all things end,
In violence, sickness, or age,

And not against that end rage,
But even the light dies.
Why then, not I?

VI.
Within the woods,
The woods within.

In each of us, a forest grows:
        deep
        dark
        stark—
A place of mysteries
    of secrets
    of madness
    of majesty
    of legend
    of magic.
We find him there,
waiting
—not patient—

Waiting for the hunt
        the chase
        the race
        and the sound of the horn.

Wild, we run,
    we hide
    we fall
    we die.

And in that darkness of death,
He is there still,
White stag, god, horned one,

Part and parcel of that forest,
>   within and without,

And as He is there,
>   in the woods,
>   >   the woods within
>   >   so are we Him.

We are He. Wild. Free.
It is autumn again.

Run.
>   Run.

The hunt never ends.
The chase begins.

Night-Blooming

Flowers never really suited you, did they?

You didn't ask to be made, woven together
from beautiful but unsubstantial stuff:
Quickly blossoming, quickly fading,
Fair of face but weak of substance,
And made by men's magic not to exist in your own right,
But to be a thing—a pretty decoration, a yielding toy,
Or at best a willing bedwarmer for yet another man.
"Wife", they might have called you,
but the name "slave" would have suited as well.

Which is to say, not at all.

It was assumed you'd be willing:
    grateful for your existence,
    grateful for any remnant of affection tossed in your direction,
    grateful to the ones who made you
        as hounds must accept the scraps tossed from master's table.

But some hounds bite the hand that feeds them,
discontented with scraps,
deeming themselves more worthy of
not just the truth of love, nor of a fairer fare,
But unwilling to accept a life in a box made ready for them:
Do this, go there, fetch that,
And always, heel!

Was it simply that you worried where Lleu's eyes might turn
once your blossoms started to wilt?
I think not:
I think that those magicians, like all men,
Conflated "wilt" with "will",

Tried to bar the slow development of one
by barring the other,
and failed.

Slow, it grew within you, this thing called desire:
    this maddened mood—
    not merely desire for another form or face in your bed,
but the desire to have your own will.
Never had they asked you what your choice might have been,
to exist as field of blossoms, or maid of radiant beauty,
    or not at all.
And if they failed to take into account this elemental question,
then surely no other desire of yours did they concern themselves with.

So, yes, desire:
The desire to be more than just some pretty man's pretty toy,
the desire to make your own choices, born of free will,
the desire to set yourself apart from him, whatever the consequences,
And so you did.

A woman's sweet voice might wheedle all sorts of interesting
    information
    from one who should know better than to divulge such secrets;
Too, a woman's sweet voice—sweeter than the nightingale,
    sweeter than the fragrance of meadowsweet—might entice
    another man
    to put good use to such secrets:
        in the moment between night and day,
        neither inside nor outside,
        neither naked as a babe from the womb
        nor clothed in king's raiment,
        not on foot and not astride,
        and with no weapon made by the hand of lawful man.

In the end, did it matter much that the one who you were made for

returned from the death that did not take him?
Did it matter much, that the one you traded him for died instead?
Did it matter much, that one of the magicians who made you
    tracked you down and changed those flowers to feathers?

After all, flowers never really suited you, did they?

Far better, the silent sweep of wing
    the strength of night-bird's claws,
    the eyes that pierce the darkness,
    the beak that pierces bone,
And better by far, the hunter's will that knows no master.

The white disc of your wide-eyed face blooms by night,
Fairer by far than the flowers of oak and broom and meadowsweet,
    —and freer, as well.

The Shores Of Greece

Gratitude

I know who to thank
for the courage to leave:
taking that first step was, after all,
the greatest journey
I would ever start out on,
the voyage that led me to freedom.

Hail, Hermes Dolios,
who helped me scheme my way
out of the hands of danger,
and keep my plans from one
who wished me ill
until it was too late for him to stop me.

Hail, Hermes Enodios,
for the road and the gift of bravery
I needed to realize
that I had to travel it.

Hail, Hermes Eriounios,
who gave me the luck to pull it off.
The path has not always been a smooth one,
but not setting out on it,
not setting the sole of my foot to
that lane both shadowed and bright
would have been a swifter trip
to Hades' kingdom
than I was willing to take.

Hail, Hermes Psychopompos,
for being willing to wait
just a little while longer
to lead me to that last gate.

Hermes At The Gate

He stands there, waiting patiently for me,
a smile on His face, hat in His hands.
There is no dust from the road on His sandals yet
as he waits for me to come out and join him:
the journey—our last one together—
has not yet begun.

Always in the past, he has traveled with me,
everywhere I went, on such long and grand voyages
as the one I made years ago to New York,
or the one before that, with my brother, as a child,
to spend the summer with my mother in North Carolina,
while she was in the army (serving under Athena's shield).

Small trips, too—a walk through the park with my dog,
watching her chase the geese while I rested
in the slant of a willow's trunk at the lake's edge,
or even just a quick trip to the grocery store,
where He would sometimes bless me with the gift
of unexpected winnings or a dollar found on the sidewalk.

But this, our last journey together—
I do not want to set out on this one,
the black road before me,
not so long as I would like it to be
(never-ending),
but coming to a stop before Hades' dark throne.

I tell myself I should not fear:
He has never let me come to harm before
on our journeys together,
but even so, I hesitate, reluctant to step out
to the gate to greet Him,

perhaps because when this voyage is over,
I will never again walk dusty back roads in the summer sunlight,
not talking, just living
—being—
with Him at my side.

Hermes In America

I.
No borders out of ancient myth and tale
Could keep Him bound up within just one land;
Swift-footed One made up His mind one day
To travel far from home and see the world.
Caduceus in hand, He hit the road—
"I've worshippers I think I'll go to see;
I'm sure they'd like a visit there from me."
The ocean was no bar to His deft feet:
Talaria to whisk Him over waves;
When He touched down, His soles were dry as bone
Baked hot in desert kiln for many years.
He cast His eyes about, grinning ear to
Ear: "Where shall I start? Who should I visit
First?" A penny glinted at His feet; He
Bent, picked it up, tossed it high in air, and
Caught it, slapped down on arm—"North it is, then,
To Boston shall I wend, and go to see
Those who love me there." And so He traveled
On, doing little tricks along the way:
A dying soul eased to the afterlife,
Stumbling speaker given tongue of silver;
Money unforeseen for a starving man.
Spreading luck and aid along the way, He
Came at last to Boston's antique byways.

II.
He walks here, has a hot dog, takes in some
History, plays with children. So much to
See, and He could spend forever seeing
It. But He has a purpose, and one by
One, He visits followers, whispering
Quietly into their ears, brushing them

With luck, smiling unseen, happy just to
Be. One woman finds a new job, out of
The blue, idiot-free, doing what she
Loves. A man skilled in Ares' ways stops near an
Alley just in time to stop a crime most
Foul. All around the city Hermes goes,
And in several of the nearby towns,
Too, sowing fortune and circumstance in
His path, before He thinks of moving on.

III.
Not far from Boston He stopped a little
While in Baltimore, murmuring words of
Encouragement and love into the ear
Of one who'd followed Him for many years.
Dark was the fog that dragged at that one's soul,
And gentle was His hand as He tarried,
Patient but firm, understanding of His
Troubles and fears, as are all lovers with
Their beloved. And when His spouse had come
To that place of calm decision, only
Then did Hermes at last turn and move on.

IV.
Wherever people worshipped Him, He stopped,
Even if just for a while, to listen
To what they had to say, to hold their hands,
To hear their sorrows and their joys. He knew
He could not stay on Earth forever; Mount
Olympus needed Him, Zeus needed Him,
But for a time, the messages would wait.
He spent a day in Memphis, another
In Alabama, spoke with a poet
In Arkansas. In Michigan, He spent
The night watching movies with an old friend,

And moved on to a girl like honey in
Colorado. Minnesota kept Him
Busy; He danced from city to city,
Savoring the time He was with each of
His children. And always He moved onward.

V.

The Midwest is wide, but His sandals were
Big enough to cross it without trouble.
Chicago took Him longest; so many
People there, calling His name, and sometimes
Not even knowing it. In one home, He
Watched a ritual to His brother, the
One whose bounteous flocks He had stolen;
The longing in the hearts of those who prayed
Was sweet as wine, and the scent of laurel
On the wind. He left them with a blessing
And a laugh, and headed on, to visit
Another, weaving through the walls of books
To brush a gentle kiss against her brow.

VI.

At last He came to stop where the salt spray
Of the Western ocean cascades into
The air, cleansing all it touches, driving
Miasma away. The sweet green scent of
Forest lingered in the air: He could feel
His sister the Huntress near, and smiled as
He headed to visit a couple who
Had held Him in their hearts for a long time.
Their prayers wreathed round His ears; their gifts brought
A smile to His eyes. He walked with them for
A day, into the woods and the hills, and
Though He never let them catch a glimpse of
Him, He knew that they understood that He

Walked at their side. Wine and bread and honey
They gave for Him. He ate, and was content.

VII.
But, in the end, He knew the time was near when
He had to return; knew Olympus would
Not wait forever. He did not wish to
Leave; friend to mankind, closest to us in
So many ways, happiest perhaps when
He moves among us unseen, but still, He
Knew He had to go. Reluctantly, then,
He bid farewell to the hills and roads He
Had traveled, said goodbye to the land that
Lay between Poseidon's waves, and once more
Launched Himself up, into the brilliant blue,
To answer duty, and His father's call.

But of course, He can never stay away.

64 Adorations for Hermes

I adore you, friend of man,
I adore you, traveler and guardian of travelers,
I adore you, silver-tongued speaker,
I adore you, guide to the final destination,
I adore you, swift-footed,
I adore you, who carries the kerykeion,
I adore you, mountain-born,
I adore you, Maia's son,
I adore you, who restored Persephone to her mother's side,
I adore you, light-fingered,
I adore you, who lent pédila to Perseus,
I adore you, father of Pan,
I adore you, whom no lock may resist,
I adore you, master of ravens,
I adore you, given to playing tricks,
I adore you, who led away Apollo's cattle,
I adore you, who waits at the crossroads,
I adore you, who stands outside every door,
I adore you, whose scepter brings sleep,
I adore you, thief at the gates,
I adore you, patron of wrestlers,
I adore you, escort for the dead,
I adore you, creator of the lyre,
I adore you, who gave moly to Odysseus,
I adore you, represented by piles of stones,
I adore you, Apollo's brother,
I adore you, lucky one,
I adore you, who brings the word of Zeus to man,
I adore you, doom of Argus,
I adore you, foe of watchdogs,
I adore you, who proclaimed his own innocence,
I adore you, thoughtful one,
I adore you, who wins every race,

I adore you, most cunning,
I adore you, who knows every language,
I adore you, speaker with bees,
I adore you, deathless one,
I adore you, who receives the sacrifices of travelers,
I adore you, son of Zeus,
I adore you, who marks every boundary,
I adore you, who guided Priam to safety,
I adore you, who sang of his own cleverness,
I adore you, who watches over the markets,
I adore you, protector of shepherds,
I adore you, who bestows charm,
I adore you, arbiter and interpreter,
I adore you, ancestor of Odysseus,
I adore you, creator of fire,
I adore you, who enters and leaves Hades' realm at will,
I adore you, lord of Arcadia,
I adore you, who gives luck to the luckless,
I adore you, patron of public speakers,
I adore you, who excels at every contest,
I adore you, who sends prophecy in dreams,
I adore you, who turned Battos to stone,
I adore you, whose voice is echoed in the rooster's crow,
I adore you, who transformed the tortoise,
I adore you, who gifted Pandora with lies,
I adore you, who speaks in dreams,
I adore you, crafty one,
I adore you, who maps out the stars,
I adore you, wanderer along every road,
I adore you, who spoke before his first day ended,
I adore you, my lord and friend.

Prayer to Hermes

Hail, Hermes Eriounios, luck-bringer, gift-giver, swift one!
To you do I give my thanks this day
for the bounty you have showered upon me.
You answered my questions and showed me the way;
Guide, watcher, keen-eyed one, I thank you.
I have gloried in the abundance you bring me,
And set my feet firmly on the path you show me.
My thanks for your guidance are unending,
And in return I give gifts back unto you.
You will not find me ungrateful, or stinting.
Let each day be a day that I say to you,
"Hail!" on the moment that I wake.

To Hermes Enodios

Setting out on journeys
always makes my heart flutter a little;
the excitement of packing, planning
my route, looking forward to whatever
awaits me at the end.
Released for just a day or two from
the boundaries that normally
circumscribe my life; I feel free
as I leave the familiar confines of home behind.
Before I go, I call your name, pour out wine,
ask You to be with me at every step—
guardian, guide, traveling companion.
I ask You to keep me safe as I travel:
safe from accidents, safe from missteps,
unharmed and whole when I reach my destination.
In my mind's eye, I can see how Your worshippers
once said the same prayers, ages ago:
the road dusty under their sandaled feet
as they trudged the well-worn paths—
to Athens, to Delphi, to Pheneos in Arcadia
where Your festivals were held.
Summer's heat haze hanging in the air,
and the bleating of goats in the fields
along their path as they made their way.
No goats on my path, but I look for Your signs
as I travel: turtle, serpent, kerykeion
splashed across the back of a truck
ferrying medical supplies from warehouse to hospital.
Midway through my trip, I will pause at a rest stop
on the side of the road and seat myself on a rock
to nibble my lunch. Then, finished, I'll
pile up smaller stones on that larger one I chose for my seat
to mark the spot where, just for a handful of minutes,

I rested in the shade of the trees overhead,
sweat spangling my brow like those old travelers,
and thought of You as they did
before resuming my journey.

All Your Faces

(Written while contemplating becoming Exegetai of Hermes.)

I see you:
Cirque du Soleil acrobat, circus aerialist,
windriding rope-spinner, sexy-sleek and infinitely nimble.
springing in wild backward flips from one end of the mat to the other.
Would that I could partake of one-hundredth such grace.

Hitchhiker, forever-wanderer,
thumb cocked backward over Your shoulder,
pointing to where You've been as You gaze
forward to where You're headed.

Craps-shooter, wheel-turner, card shark,
swift-breathed with excitement,
dogs and horses both favor You
as You ride that hot, sharp, slick streak of luck
toward the home stretch.

Sign in hand, you guide the little ones
safely across the street. Old woman or young man,
protecting the children in all their potential,
mindful of what they may someday become.

You look out of the mailman's eyes, and sail the 'netted seas;
reporter, package-bearer, gossip at the neighborhood fence—
each message that comes and goes bears Your invisible stamp.

Wry-smiling storysmith, weaving each tale,
the lines your warp and weft.
You teach me how to share what I dream,
making those worlds real with words.

And there, at the end, as I lay with eyes closed
and weighted down with coin, You wait, hand outstretched,
to take me on one last journey. With You as companion
down into the depths of Hades' realm, I shall not fear.

Enodios, Eriounious, Kourotrophis, Diaktoros,
Logios and Charidotes, Eragonios, Psychopompos.

Your names, Your faces. Someday I will know them all.

Pomegranate

Three months of winter
—oxblood and lunacy's radiance,
red harvest moonlight on snow—
Do you think his desire tempted her?
Do you think the price troubled her?
(Down into the darkness, he bore her in his arms;
Sheltered in the shadows, he lured her with his charms.)
Those ruby seeds
—glistenglimmershine with the liquid lure of vital fluids—
(his? hers? whose?)
First time, and all...
Was she really stolen from mothergoddess
(goddessmother),
Torn from green bright world
Down to night?
Or perchance
(perhaps)
It was like so many other
Loveatfirstsights:
A stranger
—as clichéd as fortune-teller's warning—
Tall, dark, handsome,
Mysterious.
His realm was no party, no swinging club, no hip crib, no cool
    crashpad.
Maybe she got bored after awhile:
He probably wasn't much of a talker,
No matter how great the sex was.
So she made up a story,
Looked for a way out.
But kidnapped? Raped?
Demeter's daughter, pretty pampered Persephone,
She who was Hades' queen?

No, she went willingly.
But she must have wanted the chance
To come back (eventually)...
Those seeds, that poppy-heart sweetness,
That reddest of reds,
Very blackest of blacks.
No accidental swallow there—
Baby, she *gulped* them down.

Demeter's Kiss

We see you in the barley with which we make our daily bread;
We see you in the joy of life that keeps our spirits fed.
You come to us when Winter ends and carry in the Spring;
You lift our hearts, enchant our minds, and teach us how to sing.

Without you, we wouldn't have sweet apples, figs, or dates;
Without you, we couldn't feed our children or our mates.
Without your love, there wouldn't be a harvest or a crop,
Without your touch upon the land, the snows would never stop.

We seek your kiss in flowers, and in vegetables and grain;
We know it is your magic that brings food from toil and pain.
We thank you for each blessing that you send us from above,
And honor you with laughter, and with incense, and with love.

When I kneel down to plant a seed, I feel you at my side;
I know you're watching as I tend my garden with calm pride.
I hope to please you with my labors as you guide my hand,
And spread your emerald bounty far across the fertile land.

Persephone's Choice

Neither choice was mine.

Put yourself in my shoes:
I wasn't precisely a child,
no matter how the stories paint things.
Sure, all the living things my mother tended
needed the help of bees and butterflies to breed,
but I wasn't wholly ignorant of sex,
not with all those nymphs around.
That was passion, yes: the grunting of satyrs
rutting in the bushes.
Birds and bees? Hah! Goats and trees.
(And streams and rocks and hills—
every naiad, oread, and dryad had a fling
with the furry little wretches.)
But love? I knew only the love
of a daughter for her mother,
and knew not how ardently I was desired.
My mother turned away all who would woo me:
the thief, the warrior, the smith, and the musician,
> keeping me to herself,
> keeping me safe,
> keeping my innocence pristine,
untouched as an ancient flower faded to grey.
dry and brittle where it lays pressed between the pages of a book.

Like the child I was, all decisions were made for me:
what and when to eat, what to wear, where to walk,
and given as much respect as might be given any powerless child:
a satisfied smile, a chaste kiss on my brow, a pat on the head.
No more had I gained for myself,
not knowing in my ignorance that more was even possible,
and no more was I due.

But He did not ask my mother's permission to court me,
knowing she would refuse the Lord of the Dead
as she had refused all others.
No, He came without warning
(a foreshadowing, if you will),
bursting up out of the earth
with all the violence and vigor
of a spear's tip, emerging from a soldier's chest
after it has been plunged into his back,
ending his life.
And thus He ended my life—
the old life of pastoral play
and picking anemones under Helios' bright gaze.
He bore me down in His arms,
raining kisses on my face,
strangely warm, for all that He is considered cold,
and strangely gentle, for all that so many of the ways
that life ends are brutal.
He wrapped me in fine silk, garlanded me with gold and rubies,
sat me on the throne next to His own,
and in one breath,
called me both "Beloved" and "Queen".

Well.

Upset as I was, frightened as I was,
it was enough to make any girl's head turn,
enough to take my breath away.
How many times had I listened
to the nymphs and the satyrs,
and wished I had arms to hold me tight, as they did?
How many times had I dreamed of hearing a dark voice
choke out my name in yearning?
How many times had I wished to pass my own hand

over the roughness of a bearded cheek?

And then there was the power to think of, of course.
My mother's bourne is life:
fruit, vegetables, grain bursting golden in ripeness,
feeding the hungry.
Apollo has music and light and prophecy and healing,
Dionysus the vine,
Hephaestus his forge,
Hermes his messages and his sly ways,
Ares his battles.
And though each and every one of them excels at his field,
those fields are limited in scope,
ending where they jut up against another's.
But everything must die—
fruits and flowers and grain,
cattle and swine and goats,
hounds and stags,
Man,
the Titans who came before us,
and yes—
even though man calls those who dwell on Olympus "the Deathless",
Yes, even gods, too, may die.
In this, my Lord is ruler over all.

How could I resist?
I knew, sooner or later, my mother
would come for me, tear me away from His side,
take me back to the fields of flowers above,
make me once again that little girl—
    without the power of choice,
    without the agency of free will,
    without He who loved me.
Neither of the first two choices were mine:
Not mine, the choice to sit in that meadow,

crowned with flowers, surrounded by nymphs.
Not mine, the choice to be torn from that meadow,
borne into the depths of the earth, worshipped by He
who rules over everything when its time has ended.
But mine was the choice to stay or to go:
this much power, I could seize.

I knew the rules: to eat would mean I must stay.
I knew watchful Helios had seen my Lord carry me away,
and what Helios knew, my mother would eventually know, as well.

The pomegranate shone like a promise.

When Hermes came to bear me back, I confessed:
these seeds, I have eaten.
And thereby bought the best of both worlds:
the joy and beauty of the meadows above,
and a mother's love.
And the embraces below, caught fast in the arms of
He whom I adore,
and that black throne.

See me now: I have made my choice,
and from that choice came all that followed.
Child no longer,
maiden no longer,
but a woman grown, and queen:
Not just beloved, but a power in my own right,
and worthy of respect.

Give me my due.

For Demeter

I kneel in the oven of the sunlight,
beating down on my back like a whip.
My hands would never win any beauty pageants—
nails broken and caked with rich soil,
they sneeringly proclaim my low interests.
I dig deep, nesting the seedling into the hole I've created,
then pack the dirt around it, gentle as a lover.
There aren't many weeds this early in the season;
nonetheless, I pinch and I pluck, nagging at the
little green things growing where they don't belong.
All around me, I can see tiny emerald shoots starting to
peep up out of the soil:
onions, corn, garlic and tomatoes,
broccoli, radishes, beets, peppers.
There are flowers on the raspberry vines and the strawberries.
At an age and circumstance beyond
bringing forth children from my womb,
still I create life.
Sweat trickles into my eyes and I wipe it away absently,
not realizing until hours later that there's a black streak smeared
across my brow.
There is nothing in my mind but
>   soil
>   seeds
>   water,
and although sometimes I don't know it,
with every breath I sing Your name.

To Demeter Erinys

Autumn is almost over, and the world inches on toward winter.
Day by day, the light fades, the earth grows colder,
and everything that once arched toward the sunlight
and flourished under my hands dies.
Apollo's light is thin and weak now,
and all the world senses the wrongness of your loss.

Demeter, I hear you weeping.

Mother bereft of child—a bargain was made,
but even though you agreed to it,
You mourn. What mother would not?
You think of her down there, cold and alone,
sitting silent at the side of her dark groom.
Does he love her? Can he? As much as you do?
What man ever loved a woman so much as her mother does?

Demeter, I hear you weeping.

This is the time of hardship: ice thickly crusted in layers
over everything, ground frozen to the bite of shovel or spade,
leaves turned colors, curled, dry, and fallen underfoot to dust.
Nothing grows. The animals that can flee the cold do,
hastening to warmer climes. Those that cannot go stay behind
and suffer. And each man and woman wraps warmer clothes
around themselves, curses the frigid chill, watches their breath
steam in the air, and waits for winter to pass.

Demeter, I hear you weeping.

No solace to think she will return in a few months;
each day apart is an agony, and the flowers refuse to bloom
at your bequest. No green buds bend the bough,

no fruit ripens, no velvet emerald grass to tread underfoot.
There is only the now of separation, the ever-present fear,
and sorrow and rage. If your eyes must redden with tears,
then so too will the world cringe and cower as sleet
whips down from the heavens, coating all the world in ice,
cold and impervious as your heart. Let Zeus know:
Uuntil she is returned, there is only frost and death.

Demeter, I hear you weeping.

Lady of the Harvest, Mother of all things that grow,
who would dare dream they have the right to command you
to dry your tears? Knowledge is no boon; even on the day
that she comes back to you at last, still the ember of grief
burns bright in your chest, for you know already that
the days will pass, too swift for comfort or joy,
before she must leave you once again.

Demeter, I hear you weeping.

Demeter, implacable one, unbending like the oak,
sharp as the scythe that cuts down the grain,
You have shown them that even she of mildest seeming
is not so easily cowed. Like a lion with her cubs,
You do not back down, nor stray from the path you have
chosen for yourself. That greatest fruit you have brought
out of your womb you protect, and in this neither
wild Artemis nor battle-wise Athena may outshine your fury.

Demeter, I hear you weeping...

...and I weep with you.

Homecoming

The price of your return is this:
to know it is never permanent.
Still, I run to meet you as you emerge from the darkness,
cloaked first in the shadows that seem to cling to you,
loving, as he can never love you,
adoring, as the whole world adored you,
stubborn, as I have been stubborn,
ready to destroy everything living
to have you by my side again.
I leap to embrace you,
one with the sun
(the sun which also leaps to embrace you,
as the grass around your ankles—
newly sprouted—
surges to hold the bare soles of your feet)
and whirl you into my arms.
The birds break into an epiphany of joy
flowers bloom where your shadow passes
(as if even that brief whisper of darkness
is fruitful, where His darkness is not)
and all the world rejoices with me.
Daughter, Kore, Spring child,
I can smell the scent of pomegranate on your lips
as I fold you to my bosom,
and it—sweet as no other sweetness
    (not honey,
    not apples,
    not the light of Helios himself)
—can ever be
is all too bitter a reminder:
In six short months, I must lose you again.
therefore, let us go now,
    down through the meadows,

    down to the riverbank,
    down where the fertile mud cakes between our toes
and wash away that darkness that clings to you
so I can pretend—at least for a little while—
that you are only and ever mine,
and I will never have to say good-bye again.

My Persephone

Today my daughter came with me into the garden,
following in the footsteps of your own child.
She knelt with me to dig holes for the peppers and the tomatoes,
packed moist earth around the roots of the cauliflower and broccoli.
I taught her about throwing away stones
that would cramp the growing potatoes,
about compost and how even things we might consider garbage
can nourish a tender, growing thing,
and about destroying parasites before they have a chance
to hurt the vulnerable babies that we work so hard to raise.
I told her about the three things that every plant needs to thrive:
warm sunlight on its face to urge it toward the sky,
sweet earth cradling its core to feed it day by day,
and water poured gently all around so it might not fade and wither.
She listened soberly, face tilted toward the green shoots
that would feed us in the months to come, understanding a little
what it means to till the earth,
to protect defenseless young living things
that cannot defend themselves, and so
in a way, she understands what it is to be a mother.

O Demeter, hear my prayer, as my daughter becomes like yours,
sitting at my side when I kneel in supplication to you
among the basil and the sage, the asparagus and the corn:
watch over her with the same dear love you bore your own Persephone,
and keep her safe until it is her time
to move on and create her own garden.

Persephone's Dilemma

After my fear faded, it was sweet in His arms—
sweet as the honey in spring
that the bees have hoarded throughout the cold winter,
curdling and clotting to pure sugar with the passing of months.
My time below was like that: dark but sweet,
and like the tiny cells of wax that the bees' children sleep in,
bereft of light.

He never meant to scare or harm me,
but after awhile, He could see how much I missed the day:
I grew wan and pale like the grass under fallen branches and stones.
I missed the flowers,
    missed the warmth of the sun,
        missed the songs of the birds and the laughter of the nymphs.
        missed, most of all, my mother's smile, the safe shelter of Her
        arms,
Her unending love.

It took a long time, but at last, She found me,
came to fetch me back to the golden world above.
My heart raced, eager as a rabbit in the lush green field,
to know the daylight again, to run barefoot over the verdant grass,
to return to my playmates
and the heady scent of bright blossoms.

But I have grown to love Him, father Zeus,
whether it is what You intended, or not,
when You gave me to Hades as bride.
His silent strength, His dark beauty,
the way He would defy You and my mother—
indeed, all the Undying Ones—to keep me at his side.
Who would not yearn for that sort of love?
I cannot turn my back on Him forever,

no matter how much I miss the sunlit lands above,
so watch now, I pray You,
as I take this pomegranate from my husband's hand,
and one by one, swallow down such seeds
as will give you no choice but to command me to return
every year to His side—
the best of both worlds, dancing in daylight above,
and embraced by Him below.
This pilgrimage, going back and forth between both my homes,
is the only choice that I can make.
Let this be our secret from my mother:
say that I swallowed the seeds, unknowing what it would mean,
for as I go home to Her now, I would not break Her heart,
But I cannot go with Her,
Leaving Him behind, alone, for all His days,
And let Her break mine.

Hard Lessons

There are certain things I am not smart enough to
Figure out the first time, Gray-eyed lady;
Basic, elemental lessons that must be repeated many times
Before they sink into my thick and insensate skull:
Don't go near crazy on the Internet,
Because you'll get it all over you and it'll never wash off;
You can't help a rabid dog, and if you try,
It'll only bite you, no matter how much you feel its pain;
What a person says isn't always a good indication
Of what he does, and only what he does is a sign of what he does;
Fool me once, shame on you, and fool me twice
—or thrice, or ten times,
Or a hundred—shame on me for being a fucking moron.

There's wisdom that doesn't come in books,
Only in getting kicked in the gut
Or in someone spitting in your face
Or people you once considered friends
Now laughing at everything you hold dear.
Ugly lessons, hard lessons, but valuable nonetheless.

Lady of wise counsel, Ageleia, Alcis, Amboulia, Paiônia, Soteira:
Protect me from my own stupidity.
Give me the strength not to turn away
from these lessons I need to learn,
No matter how much they may hurt,
And heal the wounds my heart may feel
If and when I fail to learn from them again.

Visitation

Pursued all day by owls,
In waking and in dreaming,
I knew it had to be You, Grey-Eyed Lady—
And I had counted You a friend since childhood,
But still I did not know what You wished of me this time:
So persistent,
There at every turn,
The huge-eyed stare of Your companion following me
Wherever I went.

I turned to divination to try to get an answer
About what You wanted:
Was it You, or did I just imagine meaning
Out of coincidence?
The first answer put an end to that line of thought,
And so I pushed on,
Seeking to discover
What service You wished of me.

I have always been told
I was bright, even as a youngster,
And so it was only rational
to see a connection between the two of us;
Your hand gently but firmly guided me through
Academic waters.

The rest of the questions I asked, You
Answered clearly enough even for one
Who was not so quick to see meaning in the random.
So this I swear to You:
I will do as You have asked of me,
Reach out as You have reached out to me,
And hope that, with this course of action,

You will be pleased with me,
As I have always been grateful
For the many gifts you have showered upon my head.

Lady Of The Cedars

How odd: that I thought of you each time
I breathed the scent of juniper,
but didn't know that it was your holy tree,
until I came across that reference entirely by accident.

Walking through the forest on a summer's eve,
I can see the tears of golden resin
on the outstretched branches (reaching to embrace me),
tears beyond price from the wood that weeps for your return.

Artemis Kedreatis, Artemis Hymnia,
there once was a temple at Orkhomenos
—no more than ruins now—
which I may never see; they kept your image in the crook
of a tree there, and under that tree,
your priestess might have sat, on a summer eve
not too different from this one,
smelling that sweet perfume that I smell now.

I am no virgin, nor have been for many years,
and likewise my time of childbirth is long over.
Even so, forgive me if, once in a while,
I linger by the juniper tree,
breathing in that scent,
and imagine myself joyously in service to you.

The Death Of Actaeon

He runs,
The hounds at his heels,
Head heavy with horn,
Heart heaving.

Silver light filters down through green,
Lunar radiance bleeding through
Branches of birch and beech;
He can hear their belling and baying,
See the flashing fangs.

Close, so close, too close—

Panting, he stumbles,
Panting, he falls.

In a flash, they have found him.
Teeth tearing, snarling and snapping.
Scarlet, splattered—
Meat, muscle, blood spilling over the softly-crumbling moss.

He can see her with his dying eyes,
One hand that is a hoof raised
In agony, entreating—
Her eyes hard and cold as she turns away—
Hard, cold, and as bright as her light.

What man ever suffered such transfiguration?
What child born ever grew to such rebirth?

Yet he can still recall the trembling moment
that he saw her at the spring—
Nude, gleaming, clad in moonlight and dew,

Kneeling to wash in those chill waters,
Eyes flashing in fury
As his favorite hound betrayed him with a hunter's growl.

The stag's last moan fades—
Beautiful.
So beautiful.
That accidental glance—
Death was worth it.

First Meeting

My stepmother harped on me:
come in from out of the rain, you'll catch your death of cold.
I waited until she'd gone to the grocery store
to sneak back out, the warm summer downpour
drenching me in seconds.

Barefoot, tank-top-clad, shorts pasted to my thighs by the storm,
I laughed as I danced,
whirling around and around and around
until I was drunk with dizziness, my head
swimming with it.
I sang as I danced,
laughed as I sang,
danced as I laughed,
filled with an irrepressible joy
that came from nowhere and everywhere,
throwing my face up to the sky to hear the thunder
echo laughter back at me,
the purple-grey stormclouds seeming to wear
the face of a handsome bearded man, each cloud alike.

When I spun too much, I fell, ripping open my knees on the sidewalk,
caring not at all as the blood mingled with the rain,
delirious with the giddy, breathless exaltation
welling up inside of me.

I didn't know where it came from then,
at fourteen too young and too ignorant
to recognize you as more than myth:
drunken lord, breaker of boundaries,
daring me to transgress against parental rule;
but that dance—that wild and willful dance—
was my first introduction to You,

dancing for the sake of dancing,
dancing for the joy of movement,
dancing while the rain and the warm summer breeze
danced with me.

These bones are much older now,
and I am no longer so naive and unlearned as once I was.
I have known your presence in other realms:
the sweet intoxication of wine,
the dangerous thrill of breaking boundaries set on me by others,
the maddened fury of Maenad rage,
the blinding ecstasy of coupling,
but I am not so old yet that I have forgotten you.
And so, every so often—
in the summer, when the clouds hang low
and the wind is sweet with the promise of desire,
and I hear your deep voice boom in the thunder as it nears,
I strip down to shorts and tank top,
kick off my shoes as the rain starts to fall,
and rush outside to whirl around and around and around,
dancing with you again.

To Dionysus Lyaeus
(For Sannion.)

Chain-breaker, Liberator,
    I beg your pity.
See me as I smother
    under the weight of the unasked-for
    obligations bestowed upon me
    by a thousand and a thousand more;
hear me as I groan,
    spirit breaking as I try so very hard
    to live up to what is expected of me,
    and receive nothing in return but scorn.
Feel my despair as I falter in my daily chores:
    work of hand, work of mind,
    work of heart, work of soul,
And never does the flood of tasks cease:
    bereft of joy, bereft of hope,
    bereft of rest, bereft of solace,
I trudge through each day
while others around me sing
    and laugh
    and dance
    and mock
    and jeer
    and spit.
Teach me to live as a beast of the field lives,
    free of guilt,
    free of hope,
    free of fear,
    free of loss,
knowing only the sheer simple joy of existence,
    no knowledge of the past
    no fear for the future:
exulting in each breath,

dancing with the wind,
weeping in joy at the touch of the sun's warmth on my face,
expecting nothing,
    and nothing expected of me;
demanding nothing,
    and nothing demanded of me;
requiring nothing,
    all requirements set aside.
Simply to be: free.
Haven't I done all that was asked of me, and more?
Haven't I fulfilled every duty,
    followed every law,
    given charity where needed,
    turned away from temptation,
    led a virtuous life,
    obeyed every maxim,
    broken no law,
    offered respect wherever it was due,
    honored my elders, taught my children,
    walked every extra mile?

Chainbreaker, I weary;
Joybringer, I know nothing of your gift;
Liberator, I pray you:
show me how to lay my burdens down.

My chains chafe, and I bleed:
    responsibility
    hope
    fear
    guilt
    desire
    grief.

And I see no way to be free of such chains; show me I am wrong.

Let no one say that hope cannot also be a snare:
twelve years and more I waited,
imprisoned by my heart, hoping for a change in another—
bound by hope,
> by love,
> by fear,
> by pain: pain of the heart,
>> pain of the mind,
>> pain of the flesh,
>> pain of the soul.

Twelve years, before desperation gave me the strength
> —oh, at long last!—
to break hope's chain myself, and flee.

O Lord Dionysus, breaker of boundaries, breaker of chains, I beg you:

Hear my prayer.

Eleutherus

How old was I—
fourteen, fifteen?
—that day I found myself laughing
as jagged serpents' tongues of light
tore through the indigo sky overhead
while I danced in the rain?
The sky ripped, rotten cloth strained too hard;
I was not merely wet, but drowned,
and even after my stepmother
yelled for me to come inside,
I danced on.

Since then, I have met you in
a dozen unexpected places:
bursting into song in public,
uncaring of who might hear and laugh;
dancing alone at home for the sheer
joy of the movement;
playing children's games
like hopscotch and tag and hide-and-seek
even though I have not been a child
for many, many years.

Joy-bringer, smasher of boundaries, wild one:
let the day never come when
I do not recognize your laughing, savage face,
and howsoever old and frail I may someday grow,
let me never fail to join in your games.

Apology to Hekate

I tell people I don't know you,
But that's really not true, is it?
Early on in my studies,
I heard a lot from those who I considered
Less intellectually rigorous than me,
About how wonderful you were,
>how powerful you were,
>how benevolent you were,
>how mystical you were.

Mysticism has never been an interest of mine,
Magic never something I cared to pursue.
History was what caught my attention,
And literature,
And it angered me to no end
To see those who did not even
Worship you in your proper context
Glorifying you while in the same breath
They claimed you were the very same
As Kali and the Morrigan
(And I see some similarities,
But you are not they,
And they are not you,
No matter how many people may
Believe it to be so,
Nor will it ever be, no more than
A bird is the same thing as a bat or a plane,
Simply because all three things can fly.)

So, yes, I know of you,
Although you and I have never been close,
But it is not your fault
What fools may believe of you,

So I should save my anger
For those of a fool's bent
Rather than blaming a goddess
For the deeds of her worshippers.

Therefore, I ask your forgiveness,
Prytania, Crataeis, triple-headed crone,
Mistress of the crossroads
And the hounds that howl at midnight.
Henceforth, no longer will I deny it
When folks ask if I know you,
And perhaps someday,
We might be more than strangers,
Two shades passing each other in the darkness.

Written On The Waves

I have never seen the ocean, save
as pictures in books, on TV, in film,
and yet I feel your tidal rhythms
flow through me,
too powerful to be denied.
Fearful in the way that all deep
and unexplored reaches are fearful—
abrim with strange treasure:
coral reef, pearl bank, little fish like gems
spangling those dark and liquid depths
—and you, serene and stormy by turns,
undisputed monarch
white-bearded with whitecap foam
and I, so small in comparison,
chained by unseen bonds—
(your salt tides
ebb and roar in my blood)
—can only bow in silent awe.

Adamant

Nets are not usually his forte, he thinks,
watching the shining strands slowly take shape;
weaving he leaves to Athena—
who could dream to best her at the loom?—
and earthshaker Poseidon, lord of the waves,
for who better to wield a net
then the lord of fishermen and their prey?

His normal tools—hammer, anvil, tongs—
are too clumsy for such delicate work,
each tiny golden link of the chains
—thin and imperceptible as the thread of each man's fate
before it is severed by Atropos—
gleaming in the radiance of the fire; he knots them together
with fingers more deft than many might imagine
from looking at his halting frame.

Aphrodite is *his* wife, his: he burns for her
as the fire burns for more wood,
and fury hotter than the flames of his own forge
fill his breast at the thought of her in Ares' arms.
Worse, he owes a debt to all-seeing Helios;
without that worthy's news, he would never have known.

Hephaestus lifts the finished net to the sky, the sun's
bright-burning light shining through its ephemeral weave
as if he held nothing but air; lighter than a breath,
stronger than the weighty heft of Zeus' vow,
and unseen as swift-footed Hermes when he
carries the souls of the dead to Hades' gates.

Perhaps it is from his mother that comes
this jealousy that burns as bright in his breast

as Helios' shining chariot;
all others on Mount Olympus may sport
with paramours who are not their wedded mate;
but as Hera looks with cold rage
on Zeus' many nymphs and mortal girls,
so too does he, the master of the forge,
seethe hot as molten bronze in the crucible
when again he reflects on what Helios told him.

Yes, he thinks, this should do nicely.
Folding the invisible bundle over his sinewy arm,
he heads from the forge to pay a visit
To his wife and her lover in their tryst.

Foam-Born

Here in the earliest hours of morning,
    when the birds are still sleeping
    and the beach sands glisten like tiny
    stars under their coating of sea-salt,
Here where the dawn is raw yet,
    naked with possibility,
    pregnant with potential,
You wash ashore like a pearl loosed from its oyster,
    glistening and wet under the newborn rays of
    the rising sun, and the fading
    luminescence of the sinking moon.
Here, where graceful seabirds yet slumber,
    unaware of the presence of one
    more beautiful than they, by far,
    birthed out of the opalescent seed
    of castrated Ouranos,
    mingling with the sea's salt,
    flowing forth from the ocean
    whence all life began.

As the sun rises, you unfurl from
sleep, stepping away from the scallop
that bore you to shore; most precious of blossoms,
fair-skinned, gold-tressed, eyes deep and dark
with all the desires contained there
that God or man might feel.

Swans rise in adoring worship and
beat the air with their wings,
joyfully recognizing one whose beauty
makes theirs look like lumps of coal
that look all the more filthy and misshapen
when a diamond gleams among them.

Cytherea, Ourania, Kallipygos,
Cyprian Queen:
we bow before you, stricken mute
by your perfection, and
pray you bless our dull and quiet lives
with the beauty you are known for
and the passion you inspire.
Open our hearts to the love we need
to live, to thrive, to exult in the splendor
of the world around us, and
with your grace fulfill us.

Hail Aphrodite, fierce and gentle lady!
Hail Aphrodite, forgiving and condemning!
Hail Aphrodite, love's queen!

Hades' Lament

No flowers grow in my realm.
Nor could they, even did I will it:
Helios' light cannot penetrate these depths,
nor does the sterile earth of these caverns
contain the nutrients to sustain their growth.
So my vast and dark domain held
no blush of color, no hint of light to enliven its dreary halls.

How, then, can you blame me
for plucking the rarest, most beautiful blossom of all
to brighten my drear dominion?
Am I, solely by virtue of the realm I rule,
destined to dwell alone and cheerless forever?
Am I, for all my duty and all my striving,
worth of no more than the torture of solitude,
companioned only by silent shades?
I think I have earned this small solace;
have not my battles against the Titans at
the side of my brothers earned me this much?

I loved her from the first moment I laid eyes on her.
She feared me at first, of course.
She knew me not, cosseted and hidden away by her mother,
who knew some day that blushing bud would be plucked
by some harsh and hasty suitor.
And had she known me for who I am, she might yet
have feared me more.
But perhaps ignorance and innocence
served me better, for she knew nothing of the tales that shroud me.

Not wanting to give her reason to fear me in truth,
I spoke softly to her, gently,
making of my fearsome mien something

small and harmless as a mouse's babe—
(and yet, may not even a tiny mouse bite?)
—and told her of what I hoped:
that I valued her above all things.
I whispered into her blossom-like ear
my endearments:
> beloved
>
> brightest
>
> queen

and in the end, she came to me willingly, joyfully.

In the giving of ourselves to each other,
we became part of one another,
a link forged between us, that no one—
not her mother, not mighty Zeus himself—
could sever. But despite that bond,
she could still be torn from my side...
unless those rules that part the lands of the living
from the dead
were transgressed.
And so I went to the world above long enough
to bring back a single pomegranate.

You know the rest of the story.
Even a single bite was enough to keep her at my side
for the length of half a year, every year,
despite the furious threats of her thwarted mother.
No power could take her from me forever.
And so I won.

And yet I lost;
for half the year, grief and despair and silence
cloak these halls once more,
for the fairest bud ever to bloom is absent,
and once more, I am alone.

Homecoming II

To you, the first and the last, fair Lady;
The hearth of the home,
the flame in the hearth,
the food cooking in the flame;
These things are yours,

Quiet and patient, clean and calm,
and generous, always,
giving of your hospitality
to all who come to your door,
accepting them into your home,
breaking bread with them,
seeing they are clad in garb
clean and without tear,
and giving them the best of beds
and best of pillows
on which to lay their heads at night.

You turn aside no welcome guest,
frowning only on the rude, the disrespectful,
those burdened with hubris and miasma.
And so great is your giving heart
that, when Zeus' son by Semele
came to the halls of Mount Olympus,
rather than bear a fight breaking out
among those Deathless Ones, to see
Dionysus seated there as was his due,
you willingly gave up your seat to him,
preventing loud voices raised in discord,
and claimed only the central fire to tend,
and once again sharing the best that you had
with the newly-come guest
so that He, too, might feel welcome.

Hestia, home and hearth, fire and food,
All that is welcome in the oikos:
Never shall I let your flame die out.

Helios Grieves

The horses are still now.
Here, in the West,
by the shore of the ocean
(which would boil to steam
at the touch of one amber-flame hoof),
he has brought the chariot to rest.
Even when he closes his eyes,
he can still see his son
in that last brutal moment—
trying in vain to rein the steeds in,
as the cart dove once more
to burn all the world
black as Hades' cold realm.

The other boys had taunted him,
calling his shining son a liar,
until Phaeton had begged a boon:
"So I may know beyond all doubt
that you, my father, are who you say you are,
let me drive the steeds of the sun."
The root of this day's pain:
the sun's blaze swerving, up and then down,
first bitter chill and then searing,
until at last Zeus had to act,
hurling his silver spear,
lightning bright as the sun's own gaze,
to strike his radiant son down.
there was no choice, none—
it was the right thing to do,
the proper thing,
the only thing.

Helios lets the reins fall from his grasp,

and kneels by the rocks where the sea foams,
waiting for the waves to bring his son's body home,
and weeps.

Sun God's Crown

Whose sweet leaves,
this green hair—
Where has she gone?
I saw her on that riverbank,
    lusted
    pursued
—there never was a sweeter chase—
I heard her call out her father's name.
"Save me!"
That devil, that river-god, that tyrant
—Peneius who loves not love—
whose magics these are which have
torn my Daphne away?

No woman born should dare so much,
this disappearance—
    Cassandra I punished,
    Calliope I loved,
    Coronis bore my son.
But this jewel, this prize—
How did I lose her?

I might well wear willow-weeds
(disconsolate)
But instead I gather emerald fronds,
Lovers'-token,
Almost-what if-might have been—
And weave them for my brow.
Her silk, entwined,
Not golden wreath for a locket's heart,
But verdant chaplet for my diadem:
Such hollow victory crown.

Teléia

I understand you so much better now.

The stories of the gods were written by men:
vain men, proud men, wanton and willful,
with a man's hungers, and a man's needs.
They portrayed your husband as one of themselves:
a father, a lord, a king,
with a man's hungers, and a man's needs.
Without his trysts, they say, so many Olympians and heroes
simply would not be:
>   no Apollo and Artemis, no Dionysos,
>   no Hercules, no Perseus,
>   no Persephone, no Hermes,
>   no Graces and no Muses,
>   no Seasons and no Fates

Most of the seats on the heights of Mount Olympus
would simply stand empty.

But from the first, you spurned his advances and ignored his pleas,
knowing he knew nothing of fidelity;
every gift he brought, you refused;
every flattering compliment he whispered,
you stopped your ears against.
Eventually, he sunk to trickery,
changing his shape to beguile your pity,
and only when you had brought that half-drowned bird
inside from the pounding storm laced with wild lightnings—
(and oh, if only you had recognized that warning sign!)
—he took you by force, and when he was done,
you had no choice but to wed your brother,
or live with the shame forever after.

Perhaps you thought that,

at least with the title of queen,
you could content yourself with respect, if not love,
but he made no effort to hide his affairs,
and you knew others knew of them, also.
The cloak of dignity you would have wrapped round yourself
became the cuckold-wife's tattered veil,
and all that was left to you then
were the flames of jealousy and rage
and the icy chains of hatred.

Perhaps you could understand that
the women he chose had little choice of their own—
for who could withstand the King of the Gods?
What woman could withstand his guile,
or stand fast against his strength?
Nonetheless, your fury needed a target,
and you could no more strike against him, your King,
than they could,
and so you chose to strike them down when you could—
rewarding their illicit pleasure with death if possible,
or changing their shape to something not nearly so tempting,
if your lethal hatred was balked.

Only a woman treated thusly could share
some of the anger, the despair, the hatred that you felt;
the need to strike out at the one who had hurt you so,
or, failing that, at the ones he had hurt you with.
When a woman has no such touchstone for the pain you felt,
it is easy to read the stories written by men,
and see you with clouded eyes,
thinking you spiteful or cruel,
instead of a woman seeking only the recompense of justice
for the crimes against you.

I understand you so much better now.

Incandescent

They always swear on the river Styx:
it was my undoing.
With just a few words
—the right words—
She made sure I would doubt;
mortals always do, and Hera knew
if nothing else, I was mortal:
Zeus had such a fondness for us,
fondness expressed with kisses, embraces,
and more, so much more.

So when he swore, I made my demand:
if you are who you say you are,
show me yourself in all your glory.
Oh, he begged me to change my mind:
promised me the stars and more,
but I would not relent.
He did what he could to dull his glory:
clad himself in the most meager of thunderheads,
carried the tiniest of bolts,
but it was not enough—
how could it be?
He is the Thunderer, the father of the storms, the lord of lightning,
and I nothing but human flesh,
though with a spark of something more than human
Sheltered within me.

I burned, radiant, alight the moment I beheld him,
hair a torch,
eyes molten pools of flame,
my shriek the voice of the inferno.
He did what he could—
not to save me, for I was beyond saving—

but to save the child I carried in my womb.
My heart had yet to cease beating when
he cut our babe from my flesh
and sewed him into his own.

Only then, my burden discharged, did I
fall to ash on the stones.
For more long years than I could remember
(and I could not remember, for the waters of Lethe
had washed all memory away)
did I wander among shades
as bereft of thought and memory as I,
before the gates of Hades opened to my son
who took me by the hand,
led me from that dark and shadowed place
(so unlike the light that was the last thing I had laid eyes on),
and—since he could not restore flesh
that was no longer even ash on the wind,
but memory only,
brought me up in spirit
to the majesty that was Olympus,
sharing part of his divine self
(for I had none of that;
when I carried him inside me, the
half of him that came from his father
did not transmute itself,
a mystery of will, desire, and
energy flowing between us in the aether,
through the blood that ran through both our veins),
and set me among those who dwelt there,
seated at his side,
ruling over that incandescent frenzy he induces
in the mortals whose path he crosses—
incandescent, like once I had been
in the seconds before his first birth.

Daedalus Regrets

Hindsight is everything.

I was a fool to think that, once I had built the Labyrinth,
Minos would let me go; I,
Being the only one who knew all its twists and turns, from
Beginning to end,
Was the only one who could find its center, or, from
Its center, find the way out.
And in fear, perhaps, that Pasiphae's get, that beast from her
Union with the bull,
Would follow me out to freedom, he imprisoned me in that
High tower, from which
Any fall would be instantly fatal.

But.
It was not only the paranoia of a King I had to contend with;
That bull that came from
Poseidon, powerful of sinew and gleaming white of hide,
Whom Minos' queen lusted for,
However obliquely: my hand had a role in the destruction
Of its child, as well—
For how could Theseus, no matter how crafty, how strong, how swift,
Destroy the creature
If the creature had not first been penned up within
The heart of that maze?
Twisting and turning, each path gyring upon itself, until
Even the wisest of beings,
The most patient, the most calm, could become lost and confused.
Theseus had his string,
Gift of Ariadne, to bind him to the way in and out;
The beast had no such tool.
The bull of the sun, the white bull sent by Poseidon,
Should have died at the

End of a blade, fitting gift back to Poseidon, for the sea-god's aid
In securing Minos' rule.

Minos kept the bull, fed it, housed it, loved it
Far more, perhaps,
Than he loved his wife, or loved the gods; in his anger,
Poseidon crafted his revenge;
With Aphrodite's aid, Minos lost his wife to the lust of the bull
And she bore its son.
Only after—after Minos' saw the monstrous offspring, guessed
How it came to be—
Only after the birth did the bull die, in savage and profane mockery
Of the sacrifice that should
Have been. The child he imprisoned in the Labyrinth, the maze
That I built
For him—for beast, and for King—and so by the arts of my hand
And mind, I provoked
Poseidon's wrath onto myself, as well.

The first feathers I found were of eagles; golden and strong,
Swift-winged, bright-feathered;
I collected each pinion I found, the idea blooming in my thoughts
Like poppies bloom for fair Demeter.
Wax was easy to find; at lunch each day, I requested of the servants
Of my captor
Honey in the comb to enliven dry bread and hard cheese and
Thin wine. Pitying,
They brought it; with the honey suckled free, I molded it in my
Hands, melted it with
The warmth of my flesh, embedding each feather
in a gently-curving line,
Mimicking the shape of
Eagles' wings. With string stolen from the rugs,
the bed linens, the hem of
My tunic, I tied them in line,

Watching my son play with his wooden ball, unaware; hiding my work
Each day when the servants
Returned to fetch the empty trays, watching them leave unknowing.
At length, the wings were almost
Complete; only the smaller set still lacked a few feathers on one side,
But could not soar without them,
And the eagles had not returned for days. I brooded and I stalked,
Paced and fretted, then began
Slowly to set out upon the broad windowsill a few meager crumbs
Stolen from our already
Meager meals, to attract such birds as might come hither to feast.
In time, birds came—
Not the eagles of Zeus, or the owls of wise Athene,
or the ravens of Hermes,
But a lone albatross,
Bulging belly groaning, wide white wings so vast as to shut out the sky,
And bent to the feast.
I waited until it had no care for me, beak buried in the bread
I'd scattered on the sill,
And seized it round the throat; it fought, unable to shriek, my
Hands closing its airpipe,
And at last, went limp in my grip. I had won, though my arms bled
Where its beak had struck,
Inflicting feverish gashes, filthy from its many meals. But still I
Persevered, head swimming,
Plucking such feathers as I needed to fill the final gaps, then
Casting the corpse into the sea.

I knew the albatross was one of Poseidon's creatures,
The bird of unluck,
The bird that follows ships far out into the sea,
And accursed be he
Who slays one. But I did not think of that then, as I think
Poseidon knew I would not;
All that flew and swam and roamed through the maze of my mind

Was escape.
The morning dawned bright and early as I affixed the last feather
Into its frame,
Bound it with twine, sealed it with wax, then woke my son.
I cautioned him against
Flying too high, flying too close to the bright sun's chariot, but
When has child ever
Listened to sire? We bundled them on, tightened the straps, stepped
To the sill,
Leapt.

The whole world knows how this story ends; woe that I could not
See it; I, who was called
Wisest of all men, his mind befuddled by blue sky above us, blue
Ocean below.
Young bones are swifter than old ones; Icarus quickly drew away from
Me, joyous in his
Freedom, bold in his joy, and overeager, drunk with his new toy.
Higher and higher
He flew, deaf to my warning cries, unaware as he soared so far
Above me that I
Could no longer see him; and then—oh, then—I heard his screams.
The furnace of the sun
Shows no mercy, knows no mercy for little boys; down
He fell, feathers spinning
Away from the framework, trailing droplets of molten wax—
And there, too, I wonder:
Where did that wax come from? Perhaps beehives that sat atop
A cliff, overlooking the
Blue expanse of the sea? No matter; down he fell, too fast for me
To catch him,
And I watched him plummet into the salty grave prepared for him,
Into Poseidon's embrace,
A sacrifice in place of the one the sea-lord should have had all along.
Nor did his cold clay

Wash up on the shore for me to retrieve
For proper burial.
I did not, could not, blame Apollo Helios
for his part in the matter; it is
The nature of the sun
To rise, to burn, to blaze; much like the nature of little boys
Not to listen;
How could I fault either for being what they were created to be,
When the fault was mine?
Alone, broken-hearted, I went on, to the shores of Sicily,
And in my grief
Built a temple for him who had no blame in the death,
Hung up my wings:
A final sacrifice, not to Poseidon, who had already taken
The finest gift I
Could bring him, unwillingly, but to he whom I had no right to blame:
Better I had thrown
Myself into the ocean to follow my son, given that gift doubly,
Or better still,
Refused Minos his Labyrinth
and let him pay the price that must be paid
When one offends a god.

Icarus

Up, up, into the burning blue,
nailed to the sky,
crucified, coruscating—pale alabaster icon—
where dove and raven and eagle soar.
Freedom—o Father—-
bright-mind, clever hands,
we rise on wings of dream
—feather wood wax—
(transmuted metamorphosis)
from base elements into
this bliss—
this power.
I reach out to seize white fire,
fingertips stretching toward Phoebus' face,
warmth beating down against my brow
as I chase Apollo's chariot—
too close.
Too high.
Melting, I am melting,
too full of pride, this transgression—
these molten tears drip down my shoulders
The feathers flutter away
—O Father!—
and I fall...

Calliope

(With gratitude to Neil Gaiman.)

Poetry, yes, but I've never been good at
writing you gods into fiction.
It worked only once, sort of, and
I don't look at that book much anymore.
Maybe I'm just uncomfortable
writing you into situations
that never happened
instead of waxing lyrical
about things already set down elsewhere.

But there is power in fiction—
You who are muse of epic poetry
(Iliad, Odyssey, Aeneid ... what some professors
call the first novels)
—surely understands that.
I remember stumbling across you,
O Calliope,
in an issue of a comic book, of all things,
enslaved, abused, raped, your gift of inspiration
perverted to the use of those undeserving of it
and those words, those pictures,
made me cry
even though they never really happened.

Maybe someday I will feel better about
showing the gods as characters
in a sandman's dream of never-was,
but until then, I will stick to verse.
And amusingly, unless one is a scholar,
when one hears the word 'Calliope' today,
you think not of that glorious eldest Muse

whose passion drove Homer and Arctinus and Stasinus,
but of a wild ride that goes round and round,
set to music—
which is, now that I think of it, as fitting a description
of such stories
as any other I've heard.

Where She Went Wrong

Medea,
I could almost understand your rage;
I felt it when I saw my own husband
coming out of the strip club with
lipstick on his cheek;
when he struck me because I begged him
to stop drinking;
felt it after yet another night
when he went out and didn't come home.

Medea,
I have felt that fury,
screaming at the darkest part of the night,
fists clenched, heart pounding, breath racing,
an insanity of murder pent up
and waiting to be released.

But, Medea,
you got it wrong—
those children were yours, too,
and had done no wrong.
And his new wife?
Oh, I share your wrath,
boiled with anger every time his gaze strayed,
not jealous, not wanting him still,
but to have him show me so bluntly
just how little I had ever really meant to him.
Killing Creusa and the children served no greater purpose,
save to make all the world your foe,
and wipe away in the minds of those who heard your tale
the knowledge of the wrongs done to you.

Medea—
Circe's kin, Helios' get, priestess of Hekate—
you were smarter than that,
even in frenzy.

You should have saved your knives and poison
for the guilty party.

No Distaff, No Loom

Do not fear me:
I am not any of those other weavers,
Not she who spins the thread,
Nor she who measures,
Nor the Abhorred One who severs the cord,
Nor am I Minerva, the Loom's Mistress,
Who made me thus
For my ego and my error.

Do not fear me:
My bites are not for you.
My jaws hold no poison—
(Not like that curséd coat Herakles wore)
—or, at least, no venom meant
For aught but flies and gnats.
My jaws could not stretch wide enough
To take in even the tip of
Your littlest finger.

Do not fear me:
My eight legs do not weave this shroud for you—
No distaff, no loom, no spindle,
And yet I spin;
My eight eyes do not gleam for you—
The shine in their orbs, suspiciously bright,
Comes from tears shed only for myself.
My shroud unfolds smooth and strong,
Pale as mist at dawn:
A burial shroud for my meals,
And in time, for me.

Do not fear me:
If you have it in you, pity me,

And heed the lesson I have learned:
There is nothing wrong with being proud
Of strength of thews,
Strength of mind,
Skills you have learned to make your life more pleasant,
But remember always:
There are those wiser,
There are those stronger,
There are those whose skills outshine yours
As Apollo outshines a candle,
And the gods do not appreciate your arrogance.

Do not fear me:
Should you brag endlessly about your mastery
Of this art, this craft, this talent,
Which the Immortal Gods gave you,
And to whom you owe respect, gratitude, and love,
Yet ignore them in favor of your own self-praise,
Save your fear for yourself.

In The Wake Of The Maenads

He lay strewn,
Rent,
Pieces scattered along
The Arcadian hillside,
Some of him over here,
Some of him over there
—(rather like a Scarecrow,
taken apart by monkeys)—
Blood bubbling from his lips,
The light in his eyes gone.
God's son, nightingale's voice,
Bereft.

Wandering, will-less,
Wife lost twice to darkness.
He walked with grief
Not even the music could allay.
He was warned—
They come!
Apollo's child would neither
Run nor hide,
Nor turn aside his way.
They came!
Bacchante, wine-wild,
God-maddened,
Joyous.
And so he lies,
Torn apart,
Lyre smashed, fingers broken—
Song stilled.

Solace at last, reunited
(on Death's dark, Stygian shore),

His shade searches, seeking
That tap on the shoulder,
And he turns with a soft smile:
"Eurydice..."

Abhorred

The master craftsman knows his blades, for certain:
every god and goddess that wields sword or dagger or axe
carries with him or her a piece of the lame smith's work.
But—

Hephaestus did not make *me*.
Before them all, I was:
before Zeus on his throne, and Hades in his realm,
and the siblings they share, and the mortals they rule over;
before Kronos and his sister-bride,
before Hypnos and Morpheus, before Nyx, before Gaia,
before all but Thanatos himself, I was.
My blades are sharp, and every thread I sever
tells a story I know well.
Births, weddings, children, toil:
twists in the twine, shadings of the skein.

My sisters in the hands of Her sisters take part:
the spindle pays out the thread,
and then it is measured;
but I and I alone determine when it is to end,
for without me even my wielder could not cut the cord she holds.
I am hated, I am dreaded, and yet
some earnestly long for me
to bring an end to their suffering.
I and I alone knew
that Orpheus would not bring his Eurydice out of Hades' realm,
no matter what the Dark One promised;
For had her thread not been severed?

All those heroes who thought they would live forever:
I knew better.
I do not dull; I do not rust; I do not miss;

To me, a century is as a day,
a decade as an hour,
a day as a minute,
and even as you hear this,
Know:

I will see you very soon.

Herakles Aboard The Argo

The wide-open ocean unsettled him;
The vast waves towering high as mountains during storms,
Crashing down to crush fragile human bodies against the deck.
Cold depths where sirens and nereids swam;
On land, feet firmly planted, he could tear a mountain in half,
Or—cleansing a stable that had never seen a shovel—
Shatter the course of a river, turning its route as easily
As Helios turns the horses of his sun-chariot,
Guiding it where he wills it to go.

At sea, though, nowhere firm to take a stand:
Just thin splintered planks underfoot
That would break with one stomp,
And then into the ocean's dark depths.
Even he, half-god, Zeus-fathered, can only
Hold his breath so long,
And then Poseidon's domain must win,
Salt-foam rushing into his lungs like Hera's tears of mirth.

Afraid? He would never admit fear,
But it sits snug at the core of his heart, nonetheless,
Gloating and squat and cold like a toad.
He does not know how the others cope:
Jason strides from stem to stern without apparent qualm,
Giving orders, confident and calm under cerulean skies.
But then, Jason has Hera's favor, while she has always
Denied it to him; perhaps it is easy to be calm when
The Queen of the Gods guides your hands.

His father has seldom given him special aid,
Even when jealous Hera drove him mad,
And the blood of his own children stained his hands.
Bellerophon is there, minus his famous mount;

Laertes and Medea, swift-footed Meleager and golden-voiced Orpheus,
Peleus and Telamon, always together.
If they know fear, here where death is only ever
A misstep away, they do not show it.

His fear haunts him, bringing him dreams
Of agony and flame and his favorite tunic
And his beloved wife—
But no doubt those dreams are false,
Coming to him through the gate of ivory,
And when he wakes every morning, Hylas is there
To comfort and soothe him,
And promise him, once again, that soon the voyage will be over.

King Minos's Folly

Lost within the pathless halls
—roaring panting growling—
He is so close now I
can nearly feel his maddened breath
hot on the back of my neck;
Out of the corner of my eye
I catch a glimpse of scarlet string—
Salvation! A way out of the labyrinth.
More swiftly now my footsteps echo
but it is too late—
arc of silver, and his hateful gaze:
I lift furred hands above horned head
as Theseus swings the sword down...

ΚΑΛΛΙΣΤΗΙ

Wrong.

I was wrong.

I chose wrongly.

"To the fairest." It seemed such a simple choice at the time,
And I
—so young, so smug, so full of male vigor—
knew that I was the only one to make it.
How could any other see to the crux of the choice?
There was Hera, Queen of the Gods, Zeus' bride;
There was Athena, grey-eyed wisdom, stern of countenance;
There was Aphrodite, whose beauty, unveiled to mortal eyes,
Would strike a man blind.

Well, never let it be said that I did not know
how to think with the wrong head.
Like so many before me, I let myself be swayed
by a pretty face,
too young and untried yet to know
that there were treasures greater and more worthy.

"Fairest" has so many meanings, after all:
fair of looks, yes,
but more truly, fair of judgment.
Wisdom is best in life;
beauty but a flower that fades
and is cut down long before life's end.

I look back now at that choice
so many long years ago:
rewarded with a woman promised to another,

my city in ruins,
so many lives lost,
so many betrayals.

Eris made merry twice over;
I think she knew what choice I would make,
planned not only the original dispute between the Three,
but sowed a harvest of discord and blood
that even Ares might envy.

Had I but the wisdom to have foreseen what might come of my choice,
this could have been averted;
but then, callow youth that I was,
I would not have known such wisdom
had I chosen rightly.

I am dying; this I know:
Atropos has severed my thread, and
I can count my remaining breaths
with the fingers of one hand.
The prize I once hungered for will go to my brother,
and my name will be reviled forever.
if only I had made the better choice:

Grey-eyed one, forgive me.

Other Tales

Broken Transformation

Today I wake from a dream:
I have gone raven-mad—
unsettled, eyes narrowed for anything shiny,
moving from place to place, not staying in any one spot
long enough to put down roots.

My arms and shoulders hurt and I spread them wide,
    feeling the rush of wind along the feathers I do not have,
    feeling the updrafts buoying me higher,
    feeling the warmer air caressing my jet-dark body.
My toes feel far too short—
too short to walk without falling over,
too short to curl around a branch and rest comfortably.
My mouth waters at the sight of rare meat—
barely cooked, but I would like it rarer still,
dripping with the juices that death rent from the flesh.

I make piles of glittery things that catch my eyes:
coins, buttons, pretty stones, scraps of foil,
tidying up my nest and making family and pets
wonder what I am up to.
This thick human body feels wrong, heavy, ungainly—
clumsier than it should be, the wrong shape, the wrong size.
I ache for the kiss of the sky
and the sunlight flashing across the feathers I have never worn,
and these stubby fat fingers should have ebony talons,
and in secret I weep for the sleeping life I was torn from,
and wonder how I will ever get it back.

Child of Crow

Walking, talking,
croaking, squawking—
Call me what I am, a child of Crow.
Preening my feathers,
Accepting no tethers,
Scanning the pavement so far below.

Pinion collector,
tree-branch inspector,
Eyes ever straying up toward the sun;
Swooping and gliding,
Pecking and biting,
Never afraid of a little fun.

Sharp as talons, tough as bone.
Corvid wannabe, all alone—
Looking for brethren in the blue beyond;
Sly "shinies" thief,
bold past belief—
that shadow-winged trickster of whom I'm fond.

You'll find me soaring
and ever ignoring
The fact that I don't have wings or a beak;
But still in my mind,
If I look, I find
The freedom to fly that you groundlings still seek.

Song For My Ancestors

My father was Irish and Scots, English and German,
French-Canadian and Cherokee;
My mother a heady blend of Polish, Hungarian,
Roma, Ashkenazi Jew.
His parents, and their parents, set foot on this land long ago,
settling in North Carolina,
mingling their foreign genes with those of one of
this country's original peoples.

My mother's people came over from Eastern Europe
before the Second World War;
canny folk, they saw which way the wind was blowing,
and got out—some of them, anyway—
while the getting was good.
Some days I wonder how many granduncles and aunts and cousins
I lost to the camps.

My father taught me how to fish,
My mother shared her love of gardening and herbs;
My mother's mother taught me to bake cookies
and savor the sweet, calming goodness of tea;
My mother's father showed me the value of
hard work done with your hands
—hammer a nail, measure the plank twice before cutting it—
and the serene joy of classical music.

My father's parents died before I was born,
and I know very little about them, but still
I ponder on the little things, both good and bad,
they might have left me in their genetic inheritance.
I know my paternal grandfather died of cirrhosis of the liver;
did he, as I do, love drinking just a bit more than was prudent?
My father's mother's maiden name was O'Neill,

and through her I can trace my family lineage back
to Neill of the Nine Hostages, a gift worthy of awe, indeed.

Past those two generations, I know nothing but rumor:
perhaps we are related to that Admiral Lawrence of the War of 1812:
Don't shoot until you see the whites of their eyes!
Perhaps one of my forefathers was the man who wrote
"Lady Chatterley's Lover", or the British Army officer whose
exploits in Arabia were immortalized in print and film.

I may never know, just as the ties I bear to those further back
and further still will no doubt remain a mystery to me,
until at last I pass beyond the final doorway,
to greet them in the After and speak with them at last.

I hope I have made them proud.

I hope the way I have conducted myself in life—
and, when it comes, at my death—has found favor in their eyes.

I hope I have never brought shame upon the names of those
families—blended together like the flour and eggs and vanilla
in my grandmother's favorite cookie recipe—who became my family,
and me, and that of my children.

We are the best and worst of those who came before us,
and leave the best and worst of ourselves to those who follow after us.

We are nothing without the gifts they have given us,
and the frailties, and the talents, and the flaws. No recipe is perfect;
even the best cookies may crumble, or burn in the oven, or fall.

We are each of us a melting pot.

Teind

The woods are deep;
I concentrate only on the darkness around me—
a familiar darkness, to be sure.
The forest has become my second home,
but like any family,
its gifts don't come for free.
I wince as a tangle
—wild roses, Japanese barberry,
raspberry and blackberry canes—
wrap 'round my ankles,
pierce through the denim of my jeans without much effort,
break the skin.
The forest demands its tithe of blood,
a gift for a gift,
and I give it without protest:
if blood makes the grass grow,
as the wags like to proclaim,
then it must be equally good for
oaks and hawthorns,
ash and hazel and hickory,
apple trees and maple,
motherwort and yarrow and yew.
Drink of me and share my strength, I say.
Walk through me, and share in my peace,
the woods respond.
The bargain is made,
the friendship fixed to a surety,
and I know that I am home.

About the Author

Jennifer Lawrence has been writing poetry for almost four decades now, and considers poetry, story, and song the building blocks the gods used to create the world and all that exists beyond it. A multi-trad pagan for over twenty-five years, she has followed the gods of Greece, Ireland, and the Northern lands for decades now. She is a member of The Troth, Hellenion, Ár nDraíocht Féin, and Ord Brigideach. She has worked as an editor for a small publishing company in the Midwest, centrifuge technician for a plasma company, clerk at a comic book store, RPG writer, book reviewer, newspaper editor, administrative assistant for the Academic Dean at her alma mater, and has taught writing in college at both the Bachelor's and Master's Degree levels. Her interests include history, gardening, herbalism, mythology and fairy tales, hiking, camping, and the martial arts. Her work has appeared in numerous publications, including *He Epistole*, *Idunna*, *Oak Leaves*, *Witches & Pagans*, and a wide array of devotional anthologies. She lives somewhere outside of Chicago with five cats, an ossuary and overgrown garden full of nature spirits, and a houseful of gargoyles.

www.ingramcontent.com/pod-product-compliance
Lightning Source LLC
Chambersburg PA
CBHW031142160426
43193CB00008B/223